Chinese Cooking Lessons

by Constance D. Chang

Doubleday & Company, Inc.
Garden City, New York
1978

ISBN: 0-385-12455-4
Library of Congress Catalog Card Number: 76-21508
Copyright © 1976 by Constance D. Chang
Drawings by Bunji Yoshinaga
Photographs by Kiyobumi Imai
First Edition 1977
Second Printing, 1978
Printed in Japan

Originally published by Shufunotomo Co., Ltd., Tokyo, 1976

PREFACE

Dear Readers,

These Chinese cooking lessons have been used in my cooking classes for more than 15 years. They are intended not only to teach you how to prepare specific Chinese dishes, but to tell you something about Chinese cuisine in general.

The first two Chinese cookbooks which I have published in English are "The Chinese Menu Cookbook" and "The Chinese Party Cookbook." They are designed to show how to put together a group of dishes that would be suitable for a family meal or some special occasion. This is relatively easy for most housewives and others with experience in preparation of family meals.

This cookbook is intended to be different. I have put it together according to types of ingredients—chicken, eggs, meat, vegetables, etc. The purpose of this arrangement is to instruct the less experienced on how to prepare basic materials procured from stores, and to offer ideas on what to do with food already on hand in the "fridge."

For the reason that you almost always can make appetizing dishes from food items which you already have on hand, this book should be of help. For instance, you have some eggs. Look in the eggs section for the recipe. It is as simple as that. It sometimes happens that a person will walk into the supermarket and find that, say, the cut of meat she had in mind is not up to her expectations. She has no time to shop elsewhere. What to do? She may find some other item which is on special and which is attractive but which she has not previously tried to prepare. By referring to these recipes she may easily alter her original plan so as to include such item in a different, perhaps better dish. This cookbook should, therefore, be especially useful to the young and inexperienced.

I am sure that many of you are aware of the habit of Japanese husbands to stay out late at night, eating and drinking, before returning home. On a number of occasions young Japanese brides have told me that since they learned Chinese cooking from me, their husbands are much more inclined to come home early for dinner! Of course, American and other "Western" husbands usually eat at home but, even so, preparing something different and tasty will not only make your family life more attractive and interesting but will make you more important in his life. Don't forget the old adage: The way to a man's heart, etc., etc.

I have taken this opportunity to introduce various dishes from all parts of China, both emphasizing and catering to the differences in individual taste.

It is my hope to inspire the reader to acquire a better understanding and appreciation of Chinese cookery. To this end I have included items of interest regarding the Chinese way to serve tea, table manners and other particulars concerning Chinese eating.

Sincerely yours,

Constance D. Chang

CONTENTS

Lesson 5
Fish & Shellfish

Lesson 6
Snacks & Cakes

Lesson 7
Entertainment

All recipe ingredients unavailable at your local supermarket can easily be obtained in any Chinatown or at selected specialty food stores.

REGIONAL CHINESE COOKING

The art of cooking has been a feature of Chinese life for five thousand years. The significance of this art can still be seen in the culture of present-day China.

China is a huge country with great variations in its geography and climate. The different regions have natural products unique to each as well as differing tastes which affect their cooking habits. In this section, I would like to introduce you to the various regional tastes of China.

The Eastern Region

Shanghai-style cooking is typical of dishes from this region. Seafood is frequently used, and the flavor is very heavy. Stews, using much soy sauce and sugar, are popular. Pork Stew and Sweet and Sour Pork Spareribs are well-known dishes from this area.

The Southern Region

Cooking from the city of Canton best represents the cuisine from this region. For many years Canton was a center of foreign trade, and influences from the West found their way into its methods of cooking and flavoring. Besides dishes which use an abundance of ingredients and have an international flavor. Chicken Feet-and-Mushroom Soup, Fried Beef in Oyster Sauce, Sweet and Sour Pork and Egg *Fu-yong* are representative of this region's cuisine.

The Western Region

Szechwan-style cooking well represents this area of wealth and beauty, surrounded by majestic mountains. Many prominent persons were born and raised in this area.

Because of its high humidity and cold winters, food that is spicy, hot and stimulating to the taste buds is enjoyed here. Red pepper and garlic

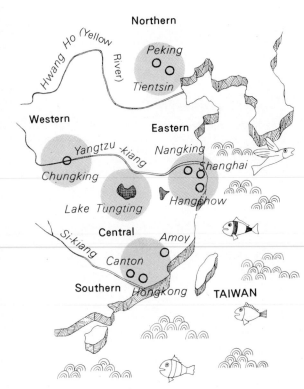

A GUIDE TO CHINESE COOKING

are often important ingredints. Fried Shrimp in Chili Sauce is a well-known dish from this region.

The Northern Region

Peking-style cooking is the dominant influence in this region. As Peking has been the capital of China for many successive generations, this select and refined art of cooking is referred to as "court cooking." Because of the cold climate, the food is rather rich in oil and salty. Peking Duck and Fish with Vinegar Sauce are well-known dishes from this area.

The Central Region

Hunan-style cooking represents this region adorned with beautiful Lake *Tungtin* in Hunan. The women in this region are renowned for their passion and grace.

Like the women, the cooking from this area features both spiciness and sweetness. Hot flavors predominate, with much use of red pepper; but bland, honey-flavored foods can also be found.

Characteristics of Chinese Cooking:

● Great variety of flavors.
Chinese dishes can be sweet 甜 and sour 酸, bitter 苦, hot 辣, salty 鹹, spicy 香, rich 肥, etc. Some taste "fresh 鮮," others are crisp-textured 脆, and still others have an aromatic bouquet 醇.

● A wide range of nutritious ingredients. In addition to fresh fish, shellfish, meats and vegetables, many dehydrated products are used. Dried foods were developed so that local foods could be transported to distant areas of the vast country.

Shark's fin 魚翅, jellyfish 海蜇, *p'i-tan* 皮蛋, gingko nuts 白果, Chinese vermicelli 粉絲 and *cha-t'sai* 搾菜 are some of the many dried or cured products associated with Chinese cooking.

● A highly developed culinary art.
There are as many as thirty different styles of Chinese cooking, from those that require only a few seconds to those needing three of four days of preparation. Chinese cooks pay careful attention to delicate changes in flavor; they study how they can make the most of the ingredients available to them.

● Special atmosphere at the table.
A typical meal finds many people seated around a large table, helping themselves to food placed in serving dishes in the center. The mood is convivial; there is plenty of food to accommodate the last-minute guest.

Deep-frying

Steaming

Stir-frying

Stewing and Braising

BASIC COOKING TECHNIQUES

Chinese cooking is based on deep-frying, frying, steaming, stewing and braising. Often the name of a Chinese dish will include a reference to the method of cooking that is to be used, so keep the following explanation of cooking terms handy for reference.

Deep-frying 炸(Cha)
●Key Point: Heat the oil quickly over strong heat. After placing ingredients in the oil, turn heat down to medium; this is important, for if the heat is too strong, only the surface will be sufficiently cooked.
Ch'ing-cha 清炸:
　　To deep-fry ingredients that are seasoned, but not coated with flour.
Juan-cha 軟炸:
　　To deep-fry ingredients that are seasoned and coated with a batter of eggs, cornstarch or bread crumbs.
Kao-li-cha 高麗炸:
　　To deep-fry ingredients coated with a mixture of stiffly beaten egg whites, cornstarch and flour. The finished product will be snow-white in color, and so this method is often used in making fried cakes. A medium-low heat is used.

Steaming 蒸 (Chêng)
●Key Point: Keep steamer hot enough to produce steam continuously. Start with high heat and later reduce to moderate.
Ch'ing-chêng 清蒸:
　　To steam ingredients which have been sprinkled with salt and pepper, then mixed with onions and ginger.
Fên-chêng 粉蒸:
　　To steam ingredients which have been seasoned and coated with rice flour.

Stir-frying 炒(Ch'ao)
●Key Point: Have a little more than enough oil to cover the bottom of the wok. Add ingredients when the oil is smoking hot. Cook quickly over a strong heat.
Shêng-ch'ao 生炒:
　　To fry ingredients unseasoned.

Ch'ing-ch'ao 清炒:
To fry seasoned ingredients with a coating of flour or cornstarch. To fry ingredients that are boiled or steamed and cut into strips.

Stewing and Braising 燒 *(Shao),* 煮 *(Chu)*
●Key Point: After bringing the water to a boil over high heat, reduce the heat, to low and simmer.
Hung-shao 紅燒:
To stew with a soy sauce flavoring.
Pai-shao 白燒:
To cook a large quantity of soup and then add salt.
Kan-shao 乾燒:
To simmer ingredients that have been previously fried until all the juices evaporate.

HOW TO PREPARE INGREDIENTS

K'uai 塊: Cube or dice

Fang-k'uai 方塊: Square or rectagular slices

Hsüan-tao-k'üai 旋刀塊: Cut into rolling cubes

P'ien 片: Slice thinly

Ssŭ 絲: Cut into strips or shred

Ting 丁: Chop coarsely

T'iao 條: Cut into sticks

Hsieh 屑: Chop or mince

Mo 末: Mince finely

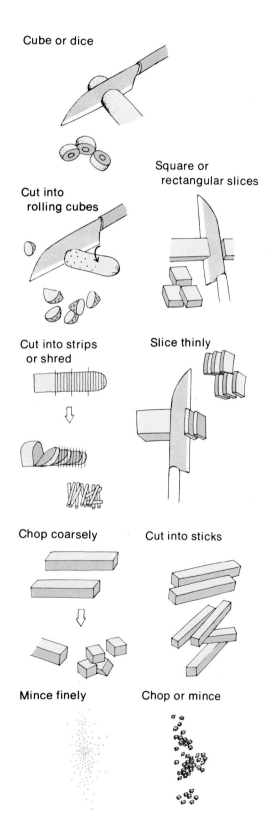

Cube or dice

Square or rectangular slices

Cut into rolling cubes

Cut into strips or shred

Slice thinly

Chop coarsely

Cut into sticks

Mince finely

Chop or mince

KITCHEN UTENSILS

The Wok: 鍋子 *(Kuo-tze)*

Used for deep-frying, steaming and frying foods. The bottom is rounded and distributes heat evenly, so that you save oil when you deep-fry.

There are two kinds of woks: Cast-iron and stainless steel. I recommend the former, because food can easily burn and stick to the bottom of a stainless steel wok.

●**Treatment for a new wok:** First fill the wok full of water and bring to a boil. Discard the water, and wipe the pan dry. Then heat the empty pan and coat it thinly with oil. After using wipe off any burnt food with a brush or a scouring pad, and wash with water. Dry completely with heat.

The Steamer: 蒸籠 *(Chêng-lung)*

Made of wood and bamboo, the steamer is flat-bottomed and shaped to fit on top of the wok. It is possible to stack several of them on top of each other. The cover of the steamer can also be used as a lid for the wok.

Do not worry about condensation ruining the finish of the steamer.

No damage will be done.

●**When purchasing your steamer;** Buy one with a diameter about 2-inch smaller than the wok.

The Ladle: 鉄杓 *(T'ieh-shuo)*

This is used when removing fried foods or soup from wok.

The Strainer: 漏杓 *(Lou-shuo)*

For lifting deep-fried or boiled foods. While carrying the food in the strainer, you can re-dip it in the oil or liquid to finish the surface evenly.

The Iron Spatula: 鉄鏟 *(T'ieh-ch'an)*

For stir-frying. The round, pipe-like handle makes the spatula easy to use. Buy the kind with a rounded edge in the front.

The Rolling Pin: 麵棒 *(Mien-pang)*

For preparing dumplings, noodles, pastry, etc. The short ones are for dumplings and the long ones for noodles.

These are the most necessary special utensils for Chinese cooking. There are many other Chinese utensils, but for these you can substitute the utensils you already have.

Wok

Strainer

Steamer

Ladle

Iron spatula

Rolling pin

TABLE SERVICE

Gold, silver and chinaware have all been used at the table in China. War lords and high officials often insisted on silverware because of a belief that silver changes color whenever it touches a poisonous substance.

In today's China, people usually use porcelain and pottery dishes. Many rare and highly prized pieces are beautifully colored in red, blue, yellow, etc.

Often, dishes can be used for both Western and Chinese foods. The following are good to have for a Chinese meal:

A soup tureen: 湯 碗 *(T'ang-wan)*
   A large, deep serving bowl for soup as well as various other dishes.

Individual soup bowls: 麵 碗 *(Mien-wan)*
   For noodle soup and boiled foods which are served with the liquid in which they were cooked.

Oval platters: 長 盤 *(Ch'ang-p'an)*
   For side dishes or fried foods. Have one large, one medium, and one small platter.

Round platters: 圓 盤 *(Yüan-p'an)*
   For fried, deep-fried and steamed foods. Again, have three in graduated sizes.

Earthen pot: 砂 鍋 *(Sha-kuo)*
   For boiled dishes. Foods cooked in this type of pot are heated slowly to a tender and full consistency. Earthenware retains heat well, so the pot should be brought to the table and the food served directly from it.

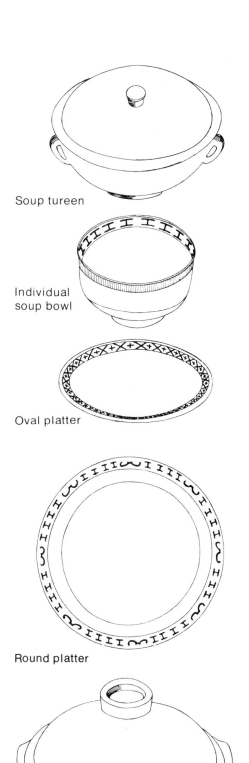

Soup tureen

Individual soup bowl

Oval platter

Round platter

Earthen pot

Perhaps you have heard the old saying, "the right man in the right place." With just a little twisting, these words could be applied to cooking: in order to enjoy the delicious flavor of chicken meat, you must know the correct way to season and cook it. In this section, we shall study the various ways of cooking chicken, using the thighs, breast and chunks of chicken as well as the whole chicken.

Lesson 1
Chicken & Eggs

▶ Chicken Casserole, p. 14

Chicken Casserole

砂鍋鶏湯 *(Sha-kuo-chi-t'ang)*

This boiled chicken dinner is best served from a tureen. The delicacy of the chicken meat and broth contrasts nicely with the vivid color and tang of the vegetables.

4 servings
1 whole chicken (about 2½ lb.)
2 green onions, chopped roughly
1-inch piece fresh ginger, chopped
2 tablespoons Chinese rice wine or sherry
2 teaspoons salt
½ lb. mustard greens or spinach

1. Clean the chicken by washing and dipping it in boiling water for one minute. Wash again with cold water. Drain.

2. Place the chicken, green onions, ginger and sherry in 8 to 10 cups of water in a tureen. Bring to a boil slowly and skim. Reduce heat and simmer until chicken is tender (1 to 2 hours). Season with salt.
3. While chicken is cooking, wash the greens and cook for 3 minutes in boiling water to which a pinch of salt has been added. Drain. Combine with the chicken and broth. Serve hot from a tureen.
4. You may serve with crackers. Keep the leftover broth for soup noodles.

Note: Monosodium glutamate (MSG) may be added to the salt as seasoning after the chicken is cooked. This is a matter of individual choice but does enhance the taste.

Fried and Wrapped Chicken Breasts 紙包鶏 *(Chih-pao-chi)*

The chicken breasts wrapped in foil are delicious and pleasing to the eye.

4 servings

½ lb. boneless chicken breasts

Mixture A:

    1½ tablespoons Chinese rice wine or sherry

    1½ tablespoons soy sauce

    ¼ teaspoon salt

    ½ teaspoon sugar

20 snow peas, washed and stringed

1 green onion, cut into thin strips

1-inch piece fresh ginger, cut into thin strips

2 teaspoons lard or shortening

oil for deep-frying

broccoli, thinly sliced, for decoration (optional)

20 pieces of alminum foil, 6-inches square.

1. Remove the white tendons from the meat and cut into 20 thin slices. Sprinkle meat with Mixture A and let sit for ½ hour.
2. Brush foil with lard to prevent chicken from sticking. Heap chicken, peas, green onions and ginger in the center and fold the edges of the foil tightly.
3. Preheat the oil to 290°F. Deep-fry the wrapped chicken for about 5 minutes. Drain. Place on serving dish. Decorate dish with the optional broccoli if desired.

15

Ground Meat and Egg Custard
肉 燉 蛋 *(Jou-tun-tan)*

4 servings
4 eggs, beaten lightly
¼ lb. ground pork
1 tablespoon chopped green onion
MixtureA:
   2 tablespoons water
   2 teaspoons Chinese rice wine or sherry
   1½ tablespoons soy sauce
   ½ teaspoon salt
   ¼ teaspoon MSG (optional)
1 tablespoon lard or shortening
2 tablespoons green peas, cooked
1 bunch of spinach
2 tablespoons oil

1. Mix together eggs, ground meat, green onion and Mixture A.
2. Grease the bottoms of the cups with lard, divide the green peas among the four cups. Pour ¼ of the meat-and-egg-mixture into each.
3. Place cups in a steamer and cover with a lid which has a hole through which steam may escape. Steam over high heat for 15 minutes.
4. While the custard is steaming, wash spinach and pat dry. Cut into three sections crosswise.
5. Heat a wok and add 2 tablespoons oil. Sauté spinach and season with ½ teaspoon of salt and spread on a serving dish. Invert teacups, removing custard onto the bed of spinach.

◀ p. 16

18

Sweet and Sour Quail Eggs with Vegetables
糖醋鶉蛋 *(Tang-ts'u-chun-tan)*

4 servings

20 quail eggs*, hard-boiled and shelled
  Quail eggs are by far the more
  preferable for this dish
2 tablespoons flour
1 carrot, boiled and cut into bite-size
  pieces
1 small bamboo shoot, boiled and cut
  into bite-size pieces
1 small onion, boiled and cut into bite-
  size pieces
1 green pepper
2 medium dried Chinese mushrooms,
  soaked in water and quartered
  (Reserve mushroom water)
oil for deep-frying
Sweet-sour Sauce:
  3 tablespoons catchup
  2 tablespoons vinegar
  2 tablespoons sugar
  2 teaspoons cornstarch
  ½ cup mushroom water
  ¼ teaspoon salt

1. Coat eggs with flour and deep-fry in heated oil. Dropping them in the oil one by one, till the color changes to a light brown. Deep-fry the vegetables in the same manner for 2 minutes. Drain on paper towels.
2. Combine ingredients for sweet-sour sauce.
3. Heat 4 tablespoons oil. Add and heat sweet-sour sauce until thick then add eggs and vegetables. Cook until heated through.

Steamed Chicken
白蒸鶏 *(Pai-chêng-chi)*

This is one of the most popular hors d'oeuvres served in China. The chicken, flavored with wine and salt, is steamed until snowy white.

4 servings

4 chicken thighs, boned
1½ teaspoons salt
1 green onion, cut into 2-inch lengths
1-inch piece fresh ginger, crushed with
  flat edge of knife
1 tablespoon Chinese rice wine or sherry
1 sprig of parsley

1. Wash the chicken and drain. Sprinkle with salt. Let stand for ½ hour.
2. Combine chicken, onion and ginger on a plate. Sprinkle with sherry and steam over high heat for 20 minutes. Remove chicken. Slice when cold. Bring liquid to a boil and season as necessary. Pour over chicken. Garnish with parsley.
3. Serve cold as hors d'oeuvre.

*
Tiny quail eggs, hardly bigger than robin's eggs, are usually used in this and the following recipe. If you cannot find them in food specialty shops or elsewhere, substitute 8 hen's eggs. The quail eggs are sometimes found canned.

Egg *Fu Yong*

Just about everyone loves "Egg Fu Yong" but not many people outside of the Chinese know from what the name derives. "Fu-yong" is a very beautiful pink and white flower (Hibiscus in English). In Shanghai, where the dish may have originated, we use only egg white and crab meat in the preparation of this dish, and the end product looks just like the flower Fu-yong. Because China is such a very large country various areas have developed their own method of preparing the Egg Fu Yong. The following are four of the principal types of Egg Fu Yong found in China. You may decide for yourself which one you prefer.

5 tablespoons oil for frying
Mixture A:
 ½ teaspoon salt
 2 teaspoons Chinese rice wine or sherry
 1 teaspoon fresh ginger juice
 ⅓ teaspoon MSG (optional)
Mixture B:
 1 tablespoon soy sauce
 1 tablespoon catchup
 ½ cup soup or water
 1½ teaspoons cornstarch
 a dash of MSG (optional)
sesame oil

Crabmeat Egg-*Fu-Yong* *Fu-Yong-Hsieh*
芙蓉蟹 *(Fu-jung-hsieh)*

4 servings
1 small can crab, cartilage removed
 and meat flaked
4 eggs
2 dried Chinese mushrooms
1 small boiled bamboo shoot
½ green onion
1 small onion

1. Soak mushrooms in water until soft, cut into strips. Cut the green onion, bamboo shoot and onion into thin strips.
2. Heat oil in a frying pan and add vegetables and salt. Cook until soft, and remove to a dish.
3. Break eggs into a bowl and lightly beat. Add Mixture A, crabmeat and the sautéed vegetables.
4. Heat more oil, add crabmeat-vegetable-egg mixture and stir-fry. Form a round shape.
5. Turn and cook the other side. Remove.
6. Stir in Mixture B, and bring to a boil. When sauce is thickened, add sesame oil. Pour over omelet.

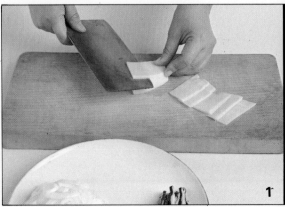

Shanghai-Style

Peking-Style

Canton Style

21

Four Variations of Egg *Fu Yong*

꡶꡶꡶꡶꡶꡶꡶꡶꡶꡶꡶꡶꡶꡶꡶꡶꡶꡶꡶꡶꡶꡶꡶

Canton-Style, Egg *Fu Yong*
芙 蓉 蟹 *(Fu-jung-hsieh)*

This style is probably the best known in foreign countries. Many ingredients are used and the dish is eaten with a thick sauce.

4 servings
1 small can crab, cartilage removed and meat flaked.
4 eggs, beaten lightly with Mixture A
Mixture A:
  ½ teaspoon salt
  2 teaspoons Chinese rice wine or sherry
  1 teaspoon fresh ginger juice
  ⅓ teaspoon MSG (optional)
2 dried Chinese mushrooms, soaked in water then squeezed dry, and sliced.
1 small boiled bamboo shoot, sliced
½ green onion, sliced
1 small onion, sliced thinly
5 tablespoons oil for frying
Mixture B:
  1 tablespoon soy sauce
  1 tablespoon catchup
  ½ cup soup or water
  1½ teaspoons cornstarch
  a dash of MSG (optional)
1 teaspoon sesame oil

1. Heat 2 tablespoons oil in a hot wok or pan. Sauté the sliced vegetables, adding ½ teaspoon salt. When vegetables begin to soften, transfer to a dish and let cool.
2. Combine seasoned eggs with crabmeat and cooked vegetables. Mix well.
3. Heat 3 tablespoons oil in a hot wok or pan and pour in egg mixture. Cook, stirring in large circles and forming a pancake-like shape. Brown both sides and transfer to a serving dish.
4. Heat Mixture B in the wok or pan. When thickened, sprinkle with sesame oil. Pour sauce over Egg *Fu Yong.*

Peking-Style, Egg *Fu Yong*
芙 蓉 蟹 *(Fu-jung-hsieh)*

4 servings
1 small can crab, cartilage removed and meat flaked
6 eggs, beaten lightly
1 tablespoon minced green onions
1 teaspoon minced fresh ginger
2 tablespoons soup or water
2 tablespoons lard or shortening
1 teaspoon Chinese rice wine or sherry
⅔ teaspoon salt
a dash of MSG (optional)
3 tablespoons oil

1. Combine all ingredients except for the oil, and mix well.
2. Heat the wok or pan to a high temperature and add the oil then pour in the crab and egg mixture. Fry until firm. Serve hot.

Shanghai-Style, Egg *Fu Yong*
芙 蓉 蟹 *(Fu-jung-hsieh)*

Shrimp Egg *Fu Yong*
蝦仁炒蛋 *(Hsia-jen-ch'ao-tan)*

In this dish there is a beautiful contrast between the yellow egg and rosy shrimp.

4 servings

1 small can crab, cartilage removed and meat flaked. Sprinkle with 1 teaspoon Chinese rice wine or sherry
5 egg whites
½ cup milk
1 teaspoon minced green onion (white part)
a dash of MSG (optional)
1 tablespoon cornstarch
4 tablespoons lard or shortening
3 lettuce leaves

1. Beat egg whites, gradually adding milk, until stiff. Carefully fold in the crabmeat, onion, salt, MSG and cornstarch.
2. Preheat wok and lightly spread lard over the hot surface. Remove wok from heat when lard begins to smoke, then pour in mixture quickly. Stir easily, in quick movements, until the mixture becomes set, You may replace the wok over low heat for a few minutes if necessary but pay close attention to the heat, being sure the eggs do not brown.

4 servings

¼ lb. shelled shrimps, washed in salt water, drained and sprinkled with Mixture A
Mixture A:
    1 teaspoon Chinese rice wine or sherry
    1 teaspoon cornstarch
    ½ teaspoon salt
4 eggs, beaten
¼ teaspoon salt
¼ teaspoon MSG (optional)
5 tablespoons oil
1 tablespoon minced green onion

1. Season eggs with salt and MSG.
2. Heat 2 tablespoons oil in a hot wok, or pan, and fry the shrimps briefly. Combine the fried shrimps and green onion with the egg mixture. Heat the remaining 3 tablespoons of oil. Add the ingredients, stirring briskly. Turn off heat when eggs are half set. Transfer to a serving dish.

Stewed Chicken Livers and Gizzards 滷肫肝 *(Loo-chun-kan)*

In China the name of this dish is "Loo-chun-kan." The word "chun" translates to gizzards, "kan" to livers. "Loo" is actually a form of food seasoning which has become institutionalized to the extent that it has become known as a method of cooking. Loo is initially prepared by combining the types of ingredients listed in Mixture A of this recipe. A very small amount of this seasoning is used in preparation of food so that there may sometimes be a quantity left over. This should not happen with the quantities provided for in this recipe, but if it should, the product can be kept indefinitely by adding to the ingredients as they become depleted through usage. There are accounts of batches of this seasoning having been retained in the families of famous gourmets for over a hundred years. The idea seems to be that the older the Loo the better it is. This may well be true.

4 servings
10 to 12 each chicken livers and gizzards,
    parboiled, fat removed
½ green onion, crushed

1-inch piece fresh ginger, crushed
Mixture A:
    6 tablespoons soy sauce
    2 tablespoons Chinese rice wine or
        sherry
    1½ tablespoons sugar
    2 tablespoons sesame oil
    1 cup soup stock
    1 star anise
    ½ teaspoon peppercorns
1 sprig parsley
1 cucumber, thinly sliced
1 small can orange slices
    and/or sweet cherries
1 small tomato

1. Place chicken livers and gizzards in an earthen pot, together with green onions and ginger, add Mixture A. Cover and simmer over low heat for 30 minutes.
2. Cool and slice livers and gizzards lengthwise. Arrange on serving dish. Garnish with parsley, tomato, cucumber, canned orange or cherries, or both.

Shredded Chicken with Chili Sauce

棒 棒 鶏 *(Pang-pang-chi)*

The highly seasoned chili sauce combines well with the light flavored chicken. This chili sauce is also good poured over Chinese noodles.

4 servings
⅔ lb. chicken breast
½ teaspoon salt
½ green onion, crushed
1-inch piece fresh ginger, crushed
1 tablespoon Chinese rice wine or sherry
1 small cucumber, cut into thin strips
⅓ lb. dried jellyfish* (optional),
Mixture A:
    1 tablespoon *chi-ma-chiang*
    1 tablespoon minced green onion
    1 teaspoon minced garlic
    ½ teaspoon minced fresh ginger
    2 teaspoons sugar
    1 tablespoon vinegar
    3 tablespoons soy sauce

    2 tablespoons chicken stock
    2 teaspoons *la-yu* or Tabasco
    1 tablespoon sesame oil

1. Sprinkle chicken with salt, let sit for ½ hour.
2. Place the chicken, crushed green onion and fresh ginger on a heatproof plate. Sprinkle with rice wine. Steam over high heat for 30 minutes. When cool enough to handle, shred.
3. Combine the Mixture A for the chili sauce.
4. Mix together the chicken, cucumbers and jellyfish. Place on a serving dish and pour on the chili sauce.

*
How to prepare the Jellyfish: The night before preparing this dish, roll up the jellyfish and slice into strips. Dip into boiling water, then soak in cold water overnight. Next morning, change the water. Before assembling the dish, rinse once more with boiling water, and let cool.

Stir-Fried Egg Yolk

溜黃菜 *(Liu-huang-t'sai)*

This dish can be prepared very quickly and is pleasing to the eye.

4 servings

6 egg yolks (these yolks may be those
 left over from previous recipe)
⅓ cup chicken broth, or shrimp water
 from previous recipe
6 canned water chestnuts, drained and
 minced
½ tablespoon cornstarch
⅓ teaspoon salt
5 tablespoons lard or shortening
2 tablespoons minced ham

1. Beat yolks slightly. Gradually add the chicken broth.
2. Add water chestnuts to the beaten egg yolks, then add cornstarch and salt.
3. Heat lard in a frying pan until vapor rises from the surface, remove pan from heat and pour yolk mixture in immediately. Mix with a spatula. If egg yolk does not properly solidify and settle in the lard, then place back on heat to increase temperature. Use care not to overheat. Transfer to a serving dish when the mixture begins to thicken. Sprinkle on the minced ham.

Steamed Egg Whites

雪花羹 *(Hsüeh-hua-kêng)*

This is a thick custardy soup with pleasant color contrasts. The leftover egg yolks, and the water in which the shrimps are soaked, may be used in the following recipe for Fried Egg Yolks.

4 servings

6 egg whites
1 teaspoon salt
1 teaspoon Chinese rice wine or sherry
½ teaspoon MSG (optional)
1 cup milk
1 tablespoon dried shrimps, soaked in
 hot water and drained. Retain water
1 slice ham, cut into thin strips
½ green onion, cut into thin strips

1. Combine egg whites, salt, Chinese rice wine, MSG, and milk in a bowl. Beat until frothy. Add shrimps to this mixture.
2. Transfer above mixture to a deep bowl. If there is any foam on surface, remove with paper towels.
3. Steam for 4 minutes over high heat. When the surface begins to thicken remove from heat. Sprinkle ham and green onion over surface and cook over medium heat for another 5 minutes.

Chicken Wings with Vegetables
貴妃鶏 *(Kuei-fei-chi)*

"Kuei Fei" in Chinese means "Empress." There was a very famous empress of the (唐) Dan dynasty who reigned about 1,300 years ago. This empress dearly loved this chicken wing dish hence the name Kuei-fei-chi.

4 servings
16 chicken wings (pour boiling water
    over them and drain)
1 bamboo shoot, cut into 2-inch chunks
4 green onions, cut into 2-inch lengths
1-inch piece fresh ginger, crushed
5 dried Chinese mushrooms, soaked in
    1½ cups water until soft, cut each in
    half (retain mushroom water)
3 tablespoons oil
Mixture A:
    6 tablespoons soy sauce
    2 tablespoons Chinese rice wine and
      sugar
    ⅓ teaspoon salt
1 teaspoon cornsatrch, dissolved in
    1 tablespoon cold water

1. Heat oil and brown green onions and ginger. Add wings and sauté until light golden color. Add bamboo shoots and mushrooms.
2. Transfer to an earthen pot or casserole. Stir in Mixture A. Bring rapidly to a boil over high heat, then reduce temperature and simmer very slowly for an hour, stirring occasionally. Add dissolved cornstarch and heat until thickened.
3. Serve hot.

Braised Chicken
新豊鶏 *(Hsin-fêng-chi)*

Hsin-fêng *is the name of a city in Canton Province. This colorful and delicious dish originated in that locality.*

4 servings
1 lb. boneless chicken cut into chunks
    and dipped in boiling water. Drained
8 canned champignons, drained *mushrooms*
3 oz. Brussels sprouts (make cross-cuts
    in bottom and parboil in water
    with a pinch of salt
1 carrot, peeled and cut into chunks
    (parboil in water with a pinch of
    salt)
⅔ teaspoon salt
a dash of pepper
a dash of MSG (optional)
1 tablespoon cornstarch, dissolved in
    1 tablespoon cold water

1. Combine 1½ cups water, chicken, Brussels sprouts, carrots and champignons in a sauce pan. Add salt and pepper. Cook over medium heat for 5 minutes, then simmer until chicken is done.
2. Gradually add cornstarch and heat until sauce thickens.

The Chinese use many kinds of meat in their cooking, but pork is by far the most common. In fact, when the Chinese say "meat," they are usually referring to pork, and so most of the recipes in this chapter will be devoted to that versatile meat.

Lesson 2 Meats

Pork Plate Stew, p. 31

PORK

Tips for buying:

Choose fresh meat that has light color, firm fat, and a certain thickness. Pork spoils more quickly than beef, so unless you plan to freeze it, do not buy more than you can use right away.

Cuts of Pork:

Fresh ham, which comes from the thigh, is very tender and lean. It is one of the most frequently used cuts of meat in Chinese cooking, often thinly sliced or cut into strips for stir-frying. Unlike many cuts of meat, fresh ham should be sliced along (not against) the grain.

Pork shoulder (shoulder butt and picnic shoulder) has more fat than fresh ham. It is also a very tender cut.

Ground pork is relatively inexpensive and can be used in a great variety of dishes. Buy it from a reliable store to be sure of its quality, and use it quickly because it spoils faster than other cuts of pork.

Pork plate is also called belly pork or fresh, un-cured bacon. It is a cut very much favored in Chinese cooking and has a distinctive flavor in boiled and steamed dishes. Pork plate consists of alternating layers of meat and fat. Its fat content is high, ranging from 45% to 68%. (Pork shoulder, in contrast, sometimes contains as little as 18% fat.) People on low-fat diets should avoid this cut, but do not ignore the recipes that call for it; simply substitute other leaner cuts of pork.

BEEF

Water buffaloes are usually the source of beef in China. Because cattle work in the fields as beasts of burden, their meat is generally tough and not as popular as pork.

Tips for buying:

Choose beef that is dark red. Bright red or pinkish meat has a poor taste. The meat will be tender if the muscle fibers are firm and closely woven and the surface of the cut is smooth. If the fibers are loosely woven and white tissues are easily visible, the meat will probably be tough. Fat is also a good indicator of quality: it should be pure white or creamy, not yellowish, and it should be marbled evenly throughout the meat.

VARIETY MEATS

Variety meats, such as liver, heart, kidneys and brains, are rich in protein, vitamins and minerals. Only one recipe in this chapter calls for a variety meat (Red-Stewed Beef Tongue), but you may substitute these very nutritious meats for the pork and beef in many of the other recipes.

Variety meats are often avoided because of their strong smell. The blending of many different flavors and foods in Chinese cooking does much to counteract this. Soy sauce, wine, bean paste, chili pepper, garlic, ginger and sesame seeds—seasonings which are often used in Chinese dishes—diminish the odor as well as enhance the good flavor of the meat.

Chinese cooks have a few simple ways to sweeten variety meats further. Before cooking liver and hearts, they place them in a bowl and pour running water over them for about 2 hours. They slice kidneys thinly, dip in boiling water and then soak them in cold water for a little while.

Pork Plate Stew
東坡肉 (Tung-p'o-jou)

Once upon a time, a famous poet named Tung-p'o *visited a temple where he smelled something delicious being cooked. "What is that wonderful aroma?" he asked. And the priest graciously answered, "It is pork plate stew, and we have been cooking it for you." This is how* Tung-p'o-jou *got its name.*

4 servings
1⅓ lb. pork plate
2 green onions, crushed
1-inch piece fresh ginger, crushed
6 tablespoons soy sauce
1 cup Chinese rice wine or sherry
4 tablespoons rock sugar
1 bunch of spinach, washed and drained
1 tablespoon oil
⅓ teaspoon salt
a pinch of MSG (optional)

1. Bring plenty of water to a boil in a large saucepan, and put in the pork. When the water returns to a boil, remove the pork. Cut into pieces, 2-inch long and ½-inch thick.
2. Put the green onions, ginger and wine in a pan. Add the sliced pork, and bring to a boil over high heat.
3. Reduce heat and pour in the soy sauce. Cover and simmer until the meat becomes tender. If the juice evaporates too much, you may add a little water.
4. Stir in the sugar. When the sugar has completely melted and the pork is glossy, remove from the heat.
5. Heat the oil, add the salt and spinach, and stir-fry quickly over high heat. Just before

removing from the stove, season with MSG. Put the meat and the sauce on a serving dish and place the spinach along one side.

Red-Stewed Beef Tongue
紅燒牛舌 (Hung-shao-niu-she)

4 servings
1⅓ lb. beef tongue
1 onion, sliced thinly
1 clove garlic, crushed
2 tablespoons oil
3 tablespoons catchup
3 cups water
Mixture A:
 2 tablespoons soy sauce
 1 tablespoon vinegar
 a little salt, pepper, and MSG (optional)

1. Wash the tongue and place in a saucepan. Pour in enough boiling water to cover the tongue completely. Cover and boil for 10 minutes over high heat. Soak in cold water for a few minutes, and peel off the skin.
2. Heat the oil and stir-fry the onion. Add the garlic and catchup, and simmer for 2 to 3 minutes. Add a dash of salt and pepper, and simmer for a bit longer. Place in a casserole (preferably earthenware).
3. Add the tongue and water to the casserole. Cover and cook over low heat until the tongue becomes tender.
4. Remove the tongue, and cut into ⅜-inch slices. Then return the meat to the casserole, and add Mixture A. Simmer for about 15 minutes.

33

◀ p. 32

1. Red-Stewed Beef Tongue, p. 31
2. Sweet and Sour Pork, p. 35
3. Steamed Pork Plate, p. 34
4. Deep-Fried Meat Balls, p. 35

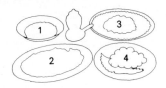

Steamed Pork Plate
白切肉 (Pai-chieh-jou)

This light dish is good for hot summer days. Serve it with several kinds of sauces and seasonings which can be used separately or combined for variations of flavor.

4 servings

⅔ lb. pork plate
1 cup Chinese rice wine or sherry
½ green onion, crushed
1-inch piece fresh ginger, crushed
cucumber slices and cherries for garnish
assorted sauces and condiments
  (see left)

1. Soak the pork in wine for 10 to 15 minutes. Drain and wind cotton twine around the meat so that it will be cooked tenderly, shaped well and easy to slice.
2. Place the meat, green onion and ginger on a heatproof plate and steam over high heat for 45 minutes or until done. (Test by sticking a skewer into the meat. Red juice will seep from the hole if the meat is undercooked; clear juice will come out if it is done.)
3. Let the pork cool. Slice and arrange on a platter with the garnishes. Serve with any sauce or seasoning that you prefer.

Sauces and seasonings:

A) Vinegar-Garlic Sauce
   Combine 2 tablespoons vinegar and 1 minced garlic clove.

B) Pepper-Salt Mix (*Hua-chiao-yen*)
   In a dry skillet, heat 10 peppercorns and 1 tablespoon salt until the salt begins to change color. Grind, or crush thoroughly with a rolling pin. A pinch of sugar and MSG may be added, if desired. Black pepperconrns may be used instead of Chinese peppercorns. Stored in a tightly capped jar, this mixture will keep indefinitely.

C) Green Onion-Soy Sauce Mixture
   Combine 1 tablespoon finely chopped green onion, a dash of salt and MSG, and 2 tablespoons soy sauce. Mix well.

D) Tomato Sauce
   Combine 2 tablespoons Worcestershire sauce and 2 tablespoons tomato catchup.

34

Sweet-and-Sour Pork
咕咾肉 *(Ku-lao-jou)*

4 servings

½ lb. pork shoulder, cut into 1-inch
   cubes
½ onion, cut into 1-inch cubes
2 green peppers, cut into 1-inch cubes
1 carrot, parboiled, cut into 1-inch cubes
2 slices canned pineapple, cut into 8
   pieces each / 8 canned cherries
oil for deep-frying plus 4 tablespoons oil
Mixture A:
   1 egg yolk
   1 teaspoon Chinese rice wine or sherry
   a little salt and pepper to taste
   1 teaspoon soy sauce
   1½ tablespoons cornstarch
   1 tablespoon water
Mixture B:
   4 tablespoons catchup
   3 tablespoons vinegar and sugar
   1 tablespoon cornstarch
   ⅔ cup water
a pinch of MSG (optional)

1. Coat the pork in Mixture A, and let sit for
   30 minutes.
2. Heat the oil for deep-frying in a wok. Deep-
   fry the pork until golden brown. Remove.
3. Quickly deep-fry the onion, green pepper
   and carrot, and remove them after a few
   minutes.
4. Heat the 4 tablespoons of oil in a clean wok,
   and pour in Mixture B all at once. Stir until
   the sauce thickens. Add the deep-fried ingredients, mixing them together. Heat
   through, and add the pineapple and cherries.
   Transfer to a serving dish.

Deep-Fried Meatballs
炸丸子 *(Cha-wan-tzu)*

Served with hua-chiao-yen *(ground Chinese
pepper mixed with salt) and catchup, these meat
balls are a delicious snack with drinks.*

4 servings

⅔ lb. ground pork
1 egg
1 teaspoon finely chopped green onion
oil for deep-frying
Mixture A:
   1 tablespoon Chinese rice wine or sherry
   ½ teaspoon salt
   1 tablespoon cornstarch
   a pinch of MSG (optional)
Garnishes: cucumber slices and cherries
Table seasonings: Tomato catchup and
   hua-chiao-yen

1. Combine the ground pork with Mixture A,
   the egg and green onion. Mix thoroughly.
   Form into 1-inch balls.
2. Heat the oil in a wok. Deep-fry the meat
   balls over medium heat until golden brown
   and well cooked. Do not fry too many at a
   time.
3. Serve on a platter with the garnishes and
   seasonings.

Deep-Fried Wrapped Beef

紙包牛肉 *(Chih-pao-niu-jou)*

You may prepare these little packages of beef early in the day, leaving only the final deep-frying for the last minute.

4 servings

½ lb. beef, thinly sliced into 20 pieces
20 snow peas, strung
2 green onions, cut into thin strips
1-inch piece fresh ginger, cut into thin strips
lard or shortening
20 pieces of parchment or wax paper
    (6-inch squares)
oil for deep-frying
Mixture A:
    2 tablespoons soy sauce
    a little salt, sugar, pepper and MSG
        to taste

1. Coat beef with Mixture A and let sit for 30 minutes.
2. Spread lard in the center of the squares of paper.
3. Place a piece of beef on the greased portion, and top with layers of green onion, ginger and snow peas.
4-A and 4-B, 5. Fold each paper into a triangle, and roll and tuck in the edges firmly so they will not open during cooking.
6 and 7. Heat the oil to 320°F. Deep-fry the packages for 3 minutes, until done. (Do not try to cook more than 5 at a time.) They are done when the paper becomes transparent. Serve in the papers, letting each person break them open with chopsticks or forks.

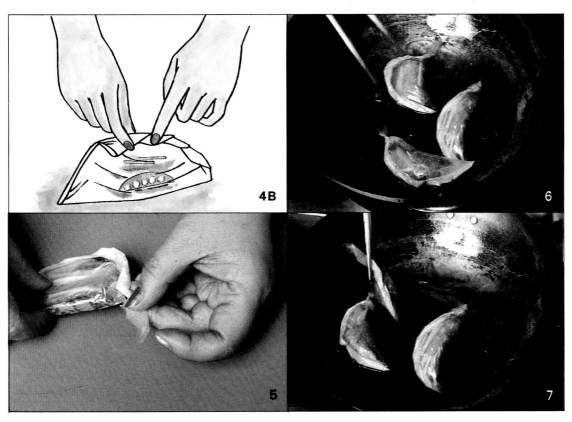

4B

5

6

7

Stir-Fried Pork and Green Pepper

青椒肉絲 *(Ching-chiao-jou-ssŭ)*

4 servings

½ lb. lean bonless pork, thinly sliced,
  then cut into strips along the grain
½ green onion, cut into thin strips
1-inch piece fresh ginger, cut into thin
  strips
½ bamboo shoot, cut into thin strips
2 small green peppers, seeded and cut
  into thin strips
5 tablespoons oil
½ teaspoon salt
Mixture A:
  2 teaspoons Chinese rice wine or sherry
  a pinch of salt and pepper
  1 teaspoon cornstarch
Mixture B:
  1 tablespoon soy sauce
  1 teaspoon sugar
  a pinch of MSG (optional)

1. Coat the meat with Mixture A, and let sit for 15 minutes.
2. Heat 3 tablespoons of the oil in a wok and stir-fry the green onion and ginger. Add the pork, stir-fry over high heat, until the color changes and remove.
3. Add the remaining oil and the ½ teaspoon salt to the same wok. Stir-fry the bamboo shoot and green peppers. Return the meat to the wok and mix, stir-frying briefly. Pour in Mixture B, and toss together quickly. Transfer to serving dish.

Stir-Fried Ground Meat and Bean Threads

肉 末 粉 絲 *(Jou-mo-fên-ssŭ)*

4 servings
¼ lb. ground pork
2½ oz. bean threads, cut into 4-inch lengths, soaked in water and drained
2 chili peppers, finely chopped
4 tablespoons oil
1 tablespoon green onion, finely chopped
Mixture A:
    2 teaspoons Chinese rice wine or sherry
    1 teaspoon cornstarch
    a pinch of pepper
Mixture B:
    3½ tablespoons soy sauce
    1 teaspoon sugar
    a pinch of salt
1½ teaspoons cornstarch, dissolved
      in 1½ teaspoons water

1. Mix together the ground pork and Mixture A. Let sit for 15 minutes.
2. Heat the oil in a wok and stir-fry the peppers and green onion over high heat. When their aroma is released, add the meat and stir-fry.
3. Pour in 1 cup of water, and bring to a boil. Add the bean threads and Mixture B. Stir briskly, then add the dissolved cornstarch and cook until the sauce thickens.

Stir-Fried Beef in Oyster Sauce

蠔油牛肉片 *(Hao-yu-niu-jou-p'ien)*

This is a famous dish of the Canton region. The oyster sauce greatly enhances the flavor of the meat.

4 servings
⅔ lb. sirloin or top round beef, thinly sliced
½ green onion, chopped finely
1-inch piece fresh ginger, chopped finely
1 teaspoon baking powder
Mixture A:
    1 tablespoon cornstarch
    2 tablespoons oyster sauce
    1 tablespoon Chinese rice wine or sherry
5 tablespoons oil

1. Dust the beef with the baking powder, and let sit for 1 hour. (Baking powder tenderizes the meat.) Then coat the beef with Mixture A, and let sit for another hour.
2. Heat the oil, and stir-fry the green onion and ginger. Add the undrained meat, and stir-fry quickly over high heat for 2 minutes.

Stir-Fried Pork with Nuts

宫保肉丁 *(Kung-pao-jou-ting)*

4 servings

½ lb. lean boneless pork, cut into ½-inch
  thick slices
½ cup shelled peanuts
½ bamboo shoot, cut into ½-inch cubes
2 red chili peppers, seeded and shredded
1-inch piece fresh ginger, sliced thinly
oil for deep-frying plus 2 tablespoons
  more oil

Mixture A:
  1 teaspoon cornstarch
  2 teaspoons Chinese rice wine or sherry
  a little salt and pepper to taste
Mixture B:
  2 tablespoons soy sauce
  1 tablespoon Chinese rice wine or sherry
  ½ tablespoon sugar
  1 teaspoon vinegar

  2 tablespoons water
  a pinch of MSG (optional)
1 teaspoon cornstarch, dissolved in
  1 tablespoon water

1. With the back of a knife, pound the thick
   slices of meat lighly, then cut into ½-inch
   cubes. Coat with Mixture A, and let sit for
   15 minutes.
2. Heat the oil for deep-frying in a wok. Quickly deep-fry the peanuts, then remove. Also
   deep-fry the meat and bamboo shoots; remove.
3. Clean the wok or use another one for stir-
   frying. Heat the 2 tablespoons of oil. Stir-fry
   the chili peppers and ginger. As soon as their
   aroma is released, add the deep-fried ingredients and Mixture B. Stir in the dissolved
   cornstarch, and cook briefly until thickened.

Family-Style Roast Pork 家庭式叉烧肉 *(Chia-t'ing-shih-ch'a-shao-jou)*

In this version of a classic Chinese recipe, the meat tastes roasted but is actually deep-fried, then simmered until done. Served cold and thinly sliced, this is a delicious cold cut; so double the recipe, if you wish, for planned "leftovers."

4 servings

1¼ lb. pork shoulder in 1 long and thin
    piece (about 8 × 1½ inches.)
4 green onions, cut into 1-inch lengths
1-inch piece fresh ginger, crushed
oil for deep-frying
Mixture A:
    2 tablespoons Chinese rice wine or sherry
    4 tablespoons sugar
    3 tablespoons soy sauce
    1 teaspoon salt
    1 teaspoon Five Spices Powder

    (Wu-hsiang-fên)
    a pinch of MSG (optional)

1. Make diagonal slits on the surface of the pork so that the marinade will sink in. If the meat is not nicely shaped, wrap it with twine.
2. Combine green onions and ginger with Mixture A. Marinate the pork for about 2 hours. Drain, reserving marinade.
3. Heat the oil in a wok and deep-fry the pork over high heat until it is deep brown.
4. Pour the marinade into a saucepan. Add the pork, and cook slowly over low heat until no liquid is left. Let the pork cool, then slice it thinly for serving.

You may roast the pork in 350°F to 450°F oven for 45 minutes, until the surface is crisp and golden brown.

Twice-Cooked Pork Plate with Hot Bean Paste

回鍋肉 *(Hui-kuo-jou)*

The pork is boiled, then stir-fried and seasoned with a special hot bean paste called tou-pan-chiang *that comes from the Szechwan region.*

4 servings

⅔ lb. pork plate
½ green onion, thinly sliced
1-inch piece fresh ginger, thinly sliced
½ lb. cabbage, cut into 2-inch squares
3 green peppers, seeded and cut about
    the same size as cabbage
1 green onion, thinly sliced on the diagonal
1-inch piece fresh ginger, thinly sliced
1 clove garlic, thinly sliced
5 tablespoons oil
Mixture A:
    1½ tablespoons *tou-pan-chiang*
        or Hoisin Sauce
    1 tablespoon sugar
    2 tablespoons soy sauce
    a pinch of MSG (optional)

1. Bring water to a boil. Add the pork, green onion and ginger to the saucepan and boil for 15 minutes. Drain. Slice the pork thinly.
2. Heat 4 tablespoons of the oil in a wok. Stir-fry the meat, and remove. Then stir-fry the cabbage and green peppers, and remove.
3. Pour the remaining 1 tablespoon of oil into the same wok, and stir-fry the garlic, the green onion and ginger over high heat.
4. When they are cooked, stir in Mixture A. Then add the pork and vegetables. Toss well, so that everything is well coated with the sauce.

Pearl Balls Coated in Glutinous Rice

珍珠肉圓 *(Chen-chu-jou-yüan)*

This dish comes from the Hupeh region of China.

4 servings

⅔ lb. ground pork
½ cup glutinous rice
1 tablespoon green onion, minced
1 teaspoon minced fresh ginger
Mixture A:
    2 teaspoons cornstarch
    1 teaspoon salt
    ½ tablespoon soy sauce
    1 tablespoon Chinese rice wine or sherry
    1 teaspoon sugar
    a pinch of MSG (optional)

1. Wash the rice well and drain. Place in a bowl and pour in boiling water until the rice is fully covered. Let sit for 10 minutes. Drain. (Do not soak the rice over 15 minutes. The rice will be sticky.)
2. Thoroughly mix together by hand the ground pork, green onion, ginger and Mixture A. Form into 8–12 balls.
3. Roll the meat balls in the rice, coating them well.
4. Transfer to a dish and place in a steamer with enough boiling water in the lower part of steamer. Steam over high heat for 20 minutes, then reduce to lower heat. The meat balls are done when the coating becomes transparent. Serve immediately.

Pickled Mustard Greens and Pork Soup

搾菜肉片湯 *(Cha-t'sai-jou-p'ien-t'ang)*

This dish is good for hot summer days. The hot flavor of the cha-t'sai *and the delicate flavor of the meat go well with the light soup. You may use bouillon cubes for the soup, but homemade stock, which you can prepare ahead of time, is much more delicious.*

4 servings

2 oz. lean bonless pork, cut into slices
10 snow peas, strung, then parboiled in
    salt water and drained (if using frozen
    ones, defrost but do not parboil.)
4 dried Chinese mushrooms, soaked in hot
    water, squeezed dry, and sliced
½ bamboo shoot, cut into slices
½ oz. *cha-t'sai*, cut into slices
5 cups stock*
Mixture A:
    ½ teaspoon cornstarch
    a little salt and pepper to taste
Mixture B:
    1 tablespoon soy sauce
    1 teaspoon salt
    a little pepper and MSG to taste

1. Coat the meat with Mixture A and let sit for 15 minutes. Then pour boiling water over and drain.
2. Heat the stock, and add Mixture B, the pork and the vegetables. Cook for about 7 to 8 minutes, until pork is thoroughly done.

Beef and Pickled Mustard Greens Soup

鹹菜牛肉湯 *(Hsien-t'sai-niu-jou-t'ang)*

4 servings

⅔ lb. rump beef, cut into bite-size pieces
3 oz. pickled mustard greens, chopped
½ lb. potatoes, cut into chunks
1 carrot, cut into chunks
2 green onions, chopped
1-inch piece fresh ginger, minced
1 clove garlic, minced
3 tablespoons oil
2 tablespoons Chinese rice wine or sherry
1½ teaspoons salt
6 cups water
a pinch of MSG (optional)

1. Heat the oil in a wok. Stir-fry the green onion, ginger, garlic, beef and wine. Add the water and cook over low heat for an hour.
2. When the meat is tender, add the salted mustard greens, potatoes and carrots. Let simmer until done, then season with salt and MSG.

*Stock: Bring 8 cups of water to a boil. Add about 1 lb. of chicken parts (use inexpensive bony pieces, such as necks, backs and wing tips). Cook over high heat until stock starts to boil. Lower heat and simmer, skimming off scum several times. For the last few minutes of cooking, add green onion and a 1-inch piece of fresh ginger to give a good flavor to the stock. Strain through a cheesecloth-lined colander.

Chinese cooking is particularly well suited to the nature of vegetables. Cooked quickly over high heat, they retain their nutritional value and fresh flavor.

Frozen vegetables should not be used in stir-fried dishes. Their water content is higher than that of fresh vegetables, and the result will be disappointingly mushy instead of crisp. This is particularly important in the case of delicate snow peas. If fresh ones are not available, substitute some other crunchy vegetable that is in season—broccoli, asparagus, or string beans, etc.

After heating the oil in the wok, you should add the salt before the vegetables. With green vegetables, the salt intensifies their color.

Lesson 3 Vegetables

44

▶ Vegetable Soup. p. 46

Vegetable Soup

素菜湯 *(Su-ts'ai-t'ang)*

A nourishing and easy-to-make dish.

4 servings
1 tomato, stemmed and halved lengthwise,
  then sliced thinly
2 cabbage leaves, cut into thin strips
½ carrot, cut into thin strips
10 snow peas, cut into strips
½ stalk celery, cut into thin strips
½ onion, cut into thin strips
6 cups chicken stock or bouillon*
1½ teaspoons salt
a little pepper and MSG (optional)
2 tablespoons oil

1. Heat the oil in a wok and stir-fry the sliced tomato. Remove.
2. Pour the stock into the wok, and add the tomatoes and sliced vegetables. Bring to a boil, then turn down the heat and simmer until the vegetables are soft. Season with salt, pepper and MSG.

*Note: See p.43 for recipe for Chinese chicken stock. If you use bouillon cubes instead of stock, taste the soup before adding salt. Bouillon cubes tend to be saltier than home-made stock.

46

Stewed Potatoes-Dumpling

素 獅 子 頭 *(Su-shih-tzu-t'ou)*

Su-shin-tsu-tou *literally means "Lion's head." The potato dumplings in this hearty dish are really large, though perhaps not quite so large as a lion's head!*

4 servings

2 lb. potatoes, washed, boiled and peeled
Mixture A:
    ½ teaspoon salt
    2 tablespoons soy sauce
    ½ tablespoon sugar
    3 tablespoons water in which
      mushrooms were soaked
    a pinch of MSG (optional)
⅔ cup flour
2 tablespoons cornstarch
4 dried Chinese mushrooms, soaked
  in water, drained and cut into large
  pieces
½ boiled bamboo shoot, cut into large
  pieces
½ cup green soybeans or peas, boiled

and shelled
Mixture B:
    2 tablespoons soy sauce
    1 teaspoon sugar
    ½ cup water
4 tablespoons oil

1. While the potatoes are still hot, mash them in a pan. Add Mixture A and mix them lightly over low heat to dry them thoroughly. Add the flour gradually, and stir until the mixture becomes stiff. Remove from the heat and divide into 4 dumplings. Dredge with cornstarch.
2. Heat 2 tablespoons of the oil in a clean wok or pan, brown the dumplings on both sides, and remove. Add the remaining oil to the pan and stir-fry the mushrooms, bamboo shoots and soybeans until cooked.
3. Place the vegetables and dumplings in a flameproof casserole, and add Mixture B. Cover and cook for a few minutes.

Stuffed Pancakes
什錦涼菜 *(Shih-ching-liang-t'sai)*

This is a festive dish that is suitable for parties. Place all the ingredients on the table, and let the guests themselves assemble their pancakes. To simplify preparations, we have used ready-made spring roll skins.

4 servings

Cut into thin strips:
  1 small green pepper, seeded (parboil
    in salt water after cutting)
  1 carrot
  2-inch length Chinese turnip
  2 lettuce leaves / 4 slices ham
  thin omelet made from 1 egg
30 agar-agar strips, soaked in warm
    water until soft, drained and cut into
    2-inch lengths
½ teaspoon salt
a pinch of MSG (optional)
2 tablespoons bean paste or Hoisin Sauce
    (available in China town)
1 tablespoon sugar
12 spring roll skins

1. Mix together the vegetables, agar-agar, salt and MSG. Place on serving dish.
2. Combine the bean paste and sugar, and add a little water. Cook until thickened, regulating the heat so that it does not scorch. (If use Hoisin Sauce omit this part.)
3. Separate the spring roll skins, and fold each in fourths. Steam until warm.
4. Place everything on the table. To eat, open up the spring roll skin, spread with a bit of bean paste, top with the vegetable mixture, and roll it up.

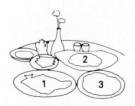

◀ See p. 48

Tomato and Cucumber Salad
蕃茄黄瓜 *(Fan-ch'ieh-huang-kua)*

The cooked sauce is poured over the salad while still hot in this light, flavorful dish.

4 servings
2 tomatoes, dipped in hot water, peeled
   and stemmed
1 cucumber, cut into ½-inch slices
Mixture A:
   2 tablespoons sugar
   2 tablespoons vinegar
   1 tablespoon catchup
   2 tablespoons water
   1 teaspoon cornstarch
a few drops of sesame oil

1. Cut each tomato into 8 wedges. Trim the cut edges of the cucumber slices, rounding them off to form a smooth surface. Place the cucumber in the center of a serving dish, and surround with the tomatoes.
2. Heat Mixture A, cooking until thickend. Add a little sesame oil. Pour the heated sauce over the vegetables.

Deep-Fried Mashed Potatoes
素炸金錢 *(Su-cha-chin-ch'ien)*

Mashed potatoes are seasoned, spread on toast rounds, and deep-fried until golden brown.

4 servings
⅔ lb. potatoes, boiled and peeled
1 carrot, finely chopped
1 teaspoon salt
a pinch of MSG (optional)
4 slices of day-old bread, cut into circles, ½-inch thick by 2-inch in diameter.
Mixture A:
   1 egg white
   1 teaspoon cornstarch
black sesame seeds
1 tablespoon parsley, minced
oil for deep-frying
garnishes (see Note below)

1. Mash the potatoes while still hot, and combine with the carrots, salt, MSG and Mixture A.
2. Cover the rounds of bread with the potato mixture. Sprinkle with the parsley and black sesame seeds.
3. Heat the oil, and deep-fry the bread with the potato mixture face down. Fry until browned.

Note: Cut a green pepper in half lengthwise. Remove the seeds, and fill with catchup. Place a mound of *hua-chiao-yen* on a thick slice of onion. Place on the serving dish with the potato rounds.

Stuffed Eggplant

茄子塞肉 *(Ch'ieh-tzu-sai-jou)*

This recipe works best with small eggplants. A variation, using a large eggplant, is also described.

4 servings

1½ lb. eggplants (about 8 small Chinese or purple ones), washed and stemmed
⅔ lb. ground pork
1 tablespoon minced green onion
Mixture A:
   2 tablespoons soy sauce
   1 tablespoon Chinese rice wine or sherry
1½ teaspoons sugar
a little pepper and MSG to taste
2 tablespoons cornstarch
3 tablespoons oil
Mixture B:
   1 tablespoon soy sauce
   1 teaspoon sugar
   ½ cup water
   a little MSG (optional)

1. Wash eggplants and remove the stems.
2. Hollow out the inside of the eggplants with a knife or vegetable corer.
3. Thoroughly mix together the ground pork, green onion, and Mixture A.
4. Stuff the meat mixture into the eggplants.
5. Dip the cut edge into cornstarch.
6. Heat the oil and sauté briefly the stuffed eggplants over high heat.
7. When they are evenly cooked, add Mixture B.
8. Cover and cook over low heat for about 5–6 minutes. Do not overcook.

Note: With 1 large eggplant, steaming works better than sautéeing. Cut the eggplant in half, scoop out the insides, loosely pile the stuffiing into 1 half and cover with the other. Place on a heatproof dish, pour over Mixture B and steam until done (about 30 minutes). To serve, cut crosswise through stuffing into 1-inch slices.

Eggplant

The Chinese eggplant is whitish, both inside and outside. It is 6 to 8-inches long and shaped rather like a cucumber. You will find this vegetable all year round at Chinese grocery stores, but you can also substitute the common purple-skinned variety, for they are similar in taste and texture. There are several kinds of purple eggplants: the large American variety, and the very small ones native to the Mediterranean region and to Japan. These small ones are frequently more tender and tasty than the larger vegetable. Sometimes eggplants, no matter what variety you are using, have a bit of a harsh taste. Soaking them in water before using will remove this.

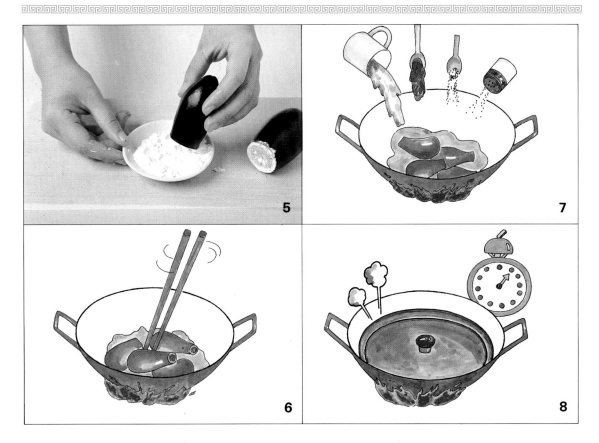

Deep-Fried Eggplant "Sandwiches"
炸茄盒 (Cha-ch'ieh-ho)

4 servings

1½ lb. eggplants (about 8 small Chinese or
purple ones), washed stemmed, and
drained

Stuffiing:

½ lb. ground pork

1 green onion, minced

1-inch piece fresh ginger, minced

2 teaspoons soy sauce

½ teaspoon salt

1 teaspoon Chinese rice wine or sherry

a pinch of MSG (optional)

Coating:

1 egg

½ cup water

½ teaspoon salt / 1 cup flour

oil for deep-frying

soy sauce-mustard mixture or catchup,
to be served with the sandwitches

1. Cut eggplants crosswise into ½-inch thick
   slices. Again cutting crosswise, make a slit
   almost through the slice so that it is hinged.
   Soak in water, and drain.
2. Thoroughly mix together the stuffiing ingredients. Insert the stuffiing into the eggplant slits.
3. Lightly beat the egg and water. Stir in the
   salt and flour, and mix well.
4. Heat the oil. Dip the stuffed eggplants into
   the coating, and deep-fry over medium heat
   until browned and thoroughly cooked. Serve
   hot with the accompanying sauces.

Stir-Fried Snow Peas and Pork
豌豆肉片 (Wan-tou-jou-p'ien)

*Unlike many stir-fried dishes, this one requires
very little advance preparation. Good to remem-
ber on busy days.*

4 servings

⅔ lb. fresh snow peas, strung

⅓ lb. thinly sliced pork

oil for frying (about 1 cup)

½ teaspoon salt

½ teaspoon sugar

a pinch of MSG (optional)

Mixture A:

2 teaspoons soy sauce

2 teaspoons Chinese rice wine or sherry

1 teaspoon cornstarch

1 tablespoon water

a little pepper

1. Coat the pork with Mixture A and let sit for
   15 minutes.
2. Heat the oil in a wok and stir-fry the pork
   quickly. Remove.
3. Leave 2 tablespoons of oil in the same wok.
   Add the salt and stir-fry the snow peas over
   strong heat.
4. Return the pork to the wok. Add the sugar
   and MSG, and pour in a little water (down the
   side of the pan in a circular motion.) When
   the snow peas soften, in about 3 minutes,
   transfer to a serving dish.

Stewed Chinese Cabbage and Mushrooms

紅燒白菜 *(Hung-shao-pai-ts'ai)*

4 servings

1 lb. Chinese cabbage, cut into
   1 × 2-inch pieces
3 dried Chinese mushrooms, soaked in
   hot water, drained and sliced (save
   the ½ cup mushroom water)
4 tablespoons oil
½ teaspoon salt
2 tablespoons soy sauce
1 teaspoon sugar
a pinch of MSG (optional)

1. Heat the oil in a wok, and add the salt. Stir-fry the mushrooms. Add the Chinese cabbage, and stir-fry again.
2. Add the soy sauce, sugar and the mushroom water. Cover and cook for 10 minutes over moderate heat. There should be very little liquid left. If there is too much, boil over high heat until the liquid is reduced. Season with MSG.

Almond Jelly

杏仁豆腐 *(Hsing-jen-tou-fu)*

4 servings

1 small watermelon
1 stick agar-agar, soaked in water and
   mashed well; water throughly
   squeezed out
2 cups water
5 tablespoons sugar
1 cup milk
a few drops of almond extract
Syrup:
   1 cup sugar
   4 cups water
   a few drops of almond extract
24 canned mandarin orange sections
12 canned cherries
2 canned pineapple slices
7 tablespoons sugar

1. Bring 2 cups of water to a boil. Tear off small pieces of the agar-agar and add to the water, cooking over low heat until it dissolves. (Agar-agar tends to boil over easily, so watch the heat.)
2. When the agar-agar is completely melted, add 5 tablespoons of the sugar, the warmed milk and a few drops of almond extract. Transfer to a rectangular container and let cool. When firm, slice into diamond shapes.
3. Boil the remaining sugar with 4 cups of water. Flavor with a little almond extract.
4. Scoop out the inside of the melon. Cut the pulp into bite-size pieces and place it, along with the other fruit, the agar-agar and the syrup, in the watermelon shell. If desired, also add the syrup from the canned fruits.

Regular bean sprouts, grown from mung beans, and soybean sprouts, grown from soybeans, are both used extensively in Chinese cooking. The regular bean sprouts are much more commonly available than soybean sprouts. If you cannot find soybean sprouts in your area, feel free to substitute the regular bean sprouts.

Lesson 4 Bean Curd & Beans

▶ Bean Curd Salad, p. 58

57

Bean Curd Salad
生拌豆腐 **(Sheng-pan-tou-fu)**

This salad is light and ideal for hot summer days. Assembled attractively, it may be served for parties as well as family meals.

4 to 6 servings

3 blocks bean curd, briefly dipped into
    boiling salt water, and drained
½ bunch spinach, boiled in salt water,
    drained and chopped
1 tomato, dipped into boiling water for 2
    minutes, peeled, seeded and thinly sliced
2 slices ham, chopped
1 oz. pickled mustard green, chopped
Dressing:
    ½ teaspoon salt
    2 teaspoons vinegar
    1 or 2 drops *la-yu* or Tabasco
    a pinch of MSG (optional)
2 tablespoons sesame or vegetable oil

1. Combine dressing ingredients with sesame oil and mix well.
2. Mash the bean curd and spread evenly in the center of a serving dish. Place the tomato slices on top, shaping them to look like a flower. Use a bit of the spinach to form a stem and leaves. Surround the bean curd with the rest of the spinach, the ham and pickled mustard green. Pour the dressing over everything.

Note: If the Chinese pickled mustard green and sauce *(la-yu)* are not available you may substitute cucumber pickles and Tabasco respectively.

How to Produce Regular Bean Sprouts

Mung beans, which are grown mainly in China and India, are green when young and reddish-black when mature. To produce sprouts, the beans are placed in warm water and set in a shady spot until the beans have doubled in size. They are then transferred onto clean sand which has been evenly spread in a tub. The beans are covered with straw, and the tub is placed in a dark place where the temperature is kept between 80°F and 85°F. The beans are removed when the sprouts have grown to a length of 2 inches.

Canned bean sprouts are a good convenience item to keep on your pantry shelves, but the flavor of fresh sprouts is incomparably better. If you cannot find them on sale, you can easily grow your own.

The regular bean sprouts are rich in vitamin C.

How to Produce Soybean Sprouts

Soybean sprouts grow considerably longer than regular bean sprouts, up to about 2 – 3-inches Cover soybeans with water and soak overnight. Drain and place the soaked beans in a colander. Cover the beans with a towel or other cloth. The beans should be kept in the colander and be watered 4–5 times daily. The watering may be done through the towel or other cloth covering the beans and the water should be allowed to drain through the colander. Continue this for 3–5 days. The bean sprouts will grow to 2 – 3-inches in length. The roots of these soybean sprouts are extremely long and should always be cut off before cooking the sprouts.

Bean Sprouts Salad
涼拌豆芽 *(Liang-pan-tou-ya)*

This is a delicious salad that has to be eaten to be believed. If the bean sprouts used are home grown be sure to remove roots and wash throughly before cooking.

4 servings
½ lb. bean sprouts, roots removed,
    washed and drained
1 teaspoon salt
1 tablespoon vinegar
1 slice ham
½ medium cucumber
Dressing:
    1 tablespoon soy sauce
    1 tablespoon sesame oil
    la-yu or mustard to taste
    a dash of MSG (optional)

1. Blanch bean sprouts in boiling water, to which vinegar and salt had first been added, then cool quickly by placing in cold water, then drain.
2. Cut the ham and cucumber into fairly thin strips.
3. Combine ingredients for dressing.
4. Place the bean sprouts on a large plate and top with the stripped ham and cucumber. Pour on the dressing immediately before serving and eating.

Bean Sprouts and Chives with Pork
豆芽韭菜炒肉絲
(Tou-ya-chiu-t'sai-chiao-jou-ssŭ)

This is a rich vegetable and meat dish that is enjoyed by virtually everyone.

4 servings
½ lb. bean sprouts, roots removed,
    washed and drained
1 bunch chives, cut into 3 sections
    lengthwise
¼ lb. pork, sliced into thin strips
Mixture A:
    1 tablespoon soy sauce
    1 tablespoon Chinese rice wine or sherry
    1 tablespoon cornstarch
    a dash of pepper
2-inch piece green onion, crushed
1-inch piece fresh ginger, crushed
5 tablespoons oil
⅔ teaspoon salt
a dash of MSG (optional)

1. Combine pork and Mixture A.
2. Heat 2 tablespoons oil in a hot wok and fry the green onion, ginger and pork, until the pork changes color. Remove from wok.
3. Heat remaining 3 tablespoons oil over high heat and add salt. Add and fry the bean sprouts quickly, then add the chives. Finally add the fried pork. Season with the MSG, if used, and transfer to a serving dish.

Something about Soybeans

Soybean cultivation originated in China. The soybean is an annual of the bean family. There are as many as 300 different varieties of the soybean plant.

Soybeans are highly nutritious. Because of their high protein content they have sometimes been called the "meat of the fields." A number of research organizations are experimenting with soybeans in the production of meat substitutes which closely resemble beef derivatives such as hamburger and even steak. The resemblance is said to be remarkable, not only as to appearance but also taste. Many experts believe that soybeans will play a paramount role in feeding tomorrow's multitudes if and when the world food situation becomes critical. In addition to the protein content, soybeans contain vitamins and some sugar and fat. Linoleic and linolenic acids are present in the fat. Soybeans are alkaline and very good for the health.

Bean curd, produced from soybeans and treated elsewhere in this book, is actually a soybean concentrate and has enormous nutrient value.

Large beans are used in the manufacture of soy sauce, bean paste, soybean milk, bean curd, dried bean curd and fermented beans. Smaller beans are used to make oil, soybean flour, cakes and bean sprouts.

Not fully ripened (green) soybeans are a good snack with drinks. To make these, first boil in the pod, with salt, until tender but still crisp, drain, cool rapidly under cold running water. Serve in the pod. One should suck the beans out and discard the pod.

Meatball and Soybean Stew

黄豆肉圓 *(Huang-tou-jou-yüan)*

4 servings

1 cup soybeans, washed and soaked in
  water overnight
⅔ lb. ground pork
1 egg
1 tablespoon minced green onion
1 teaspoon minced fresh ginger
1 tablespoon cornstarch
Mixture A:
  1 tablespoon Chinese rice wine or sherry
  1 tablespoon soy sauce
  a pinch of salt and pepper
  a pinch of MSG (optional)
oil for deep-frying
Mixture B:
  2 tablespoons soy sauce
  1 teaspoon sugar
  2 cups water

1. Thoroughly mix the ground meat, egg, green onion, ginger, cornstarch and Mixture A. Form 10 to 15 meatballs.
2. Heat the oil in a wok. Deep-fry the meatballs until brown, scoop out and drain.
3. Place the soybeans in a deep pot and add Mixture B. Simmer over a moderate heat. When the soybeans begin to soften, add the deep-fried meatballs, cover, reduce heat and simmer.
4. The stew is done when the soybeans become very soft. Some cooks let the stew simmer so long that the beans actually "melt." Try both ways and see which one your prefer.

Fried Soybeans

油炸黃豆 *(Yu-cha-huang-tou)*

This is a crisp and flavorful snack, ideal for serving with drinks. Sometimes it is eaten with porridge. In America, roasted soybeans are also used as a snack, or side dish with hors-d'oeuvre.

4 servings

1 cup soybeans
oil for deep-frying
1 tablespoon salt

1. Prepare well ahead of time needed.
2. Soak soybeans in water overnight. Drain thoroughly and place in a colander or bamboo bowl to dry slowly in the sun. (Sun drying makes the beans turn out very crispy).
3. Heat oil to 320°F. Deep-fry the dried beans slowly, stirring occasionally until golden in color. Fry slowly, so as not to scorch the beans.
4. Scoop beans from oil with a slotted spoon and place on paper towels to drain. Sprinkle with salt while still hot.

Note: Peanuts can be used instead of soybeans in the preparation of this snack.

Soybean Milk and Its Uses

豆腐漿 *(Tou-fu-chiang)*

During the early stages of making bean curd, a highly nutritious milky liquid is produced. You can produce this "milk" in a blender and serve it as a between-meal refresher.

4 servings

1 cup soybeans, soaked in water overnight, then drained
3 to 4 cups water
flavoring of your choice (sugar, cocoa, coffee, etc.)

Grind soybeans in a blender, adding a little bit of water. Mix until the beans are reduced to a fine pulp. Add remaining water. Pour into a cheesecloth-lined colander which has been placed over a bowl. Wrap the cheesecloth over the bean pulp and extract all the milk by squeezing and wringing.

2. Pour the milk into a saucepan and bring to a boil. Serve hot or cold, flavored with sugar and cocoa or coffee.

Bean Curd and How to Make It

Bean curd is made from the milk of soybeans. It is somewhat difficult to make at home. If you wish to try, the easiest way is to buy a box of bean curd powder in a Japanese food store and follow the instructions. You can make a very good bean curd at home once you master the technique.

Bean curd is a true health food. It is high in protein and low in fats and carbohydrates. It contains a generous amount of potassium, some calcium, phosphorus and iron, and small amounts of vitamins (A, B_1, B_2, C).

Bean curd is highly perishable. It will keep for 2–3 days if you place it in water and store in the refrigerator. It will stay fresh for a day or two longer if you change the water occasionally. On the other hand bean curd can be deep-fried, pressed and frozen, in which case it will keep indefinitely.

Bean curd is a ready-to-eat food and can be served hot or cold, cooked or uncooked. However, if you plan to eat it uncooked, take the precaution of first dipping it in boiling water to destroy the germs that sometimes collect on the surface.

A great many if not most of the Chinese people obtain their necessary daily protein from this wonderful bean curd.

You can find bean curd in oriental food stores. In Chinese stores, bean curd will be called "tou-fu" or "dow-fu"; in Japanese stores, ask for "tofu."

Bean curd can be safely retained on hand indefinitely by the simple expedient of freezing in your home freezer, or freezer compartment of the refrigerator. You may put one or two blocks of bean curd in the freezer compartment and freeze overnight or until they become hard. When you wish to use the bean curd simply pour boiling water over and pat dry. The frozen bean curd develops an unusual and interesting spongy texture which facilitates slicing into thin pieces which may be used as an ingredient in soups, stews, etc.

Spicybean Curd and Pork
麻婆豆腐 (Ma-p'o-tou-fu)

This is a famous Szechwan style dish which was created by an old lady named Chen about 400 years ago in China. This dish has become very famous worldwide and Mrs. Chen can be justly proud of herself in heaven.

4 servings
2 blocks bean curd, cut into 1-inch cubes, dipped into boiling water and drained
¼ lb. ground pork
3 tablespoons oil
2 teaspoons *la-chiang* (red pepper paste)
2 tablespoons soy sauce
½ cup broth or water
1 green onion, chopped
1 clove garlic, minced
1 – 2 tablespoons cornstarch, dissolved in double the amount of water
a pinch of salt
a pinch of MSG (optional)
a few drops of sesame oil

1. Heat an empty wok then add the oil, green onion, garlic, stir gently, then add ground meat. When the pork is well cooked, add the *la-chiang* and broth. Mix well. Add bean curd and soy sauce, bring to a boil then season with salt and MSG. Reduce the heat, cover and cook for 3 minutes.
2. Pour in the dissolved cornstarch, mixing well. Pour in a few drops of sesame oil and serve immediately.

Home-Style Bean Curd Stew   家常豆腐 *(Chia-ch'ang-tou-fu)*

This is a bit hot flavored and goes well with plain rice or bread.

4 servings

1 block bean curd, sliced into ½ -inch strips
5 oz. thinly sliced pork shoulder, cut into
   bite-size squares
Mixture A:
   1 tablespoon soy sauce
   1 teaspoon cornstarch
   1 teaspoon Chinese rice wine or sherry
1 green pepper, cut into chunks
2 chili peppers, minced
3 dried Chinese mushrooms, soaked
   in water until soft, drained and cut
   into chunks (reserve mushroom water)
1 boiled bamboo shoot, cut into chunks
Mixture B:
   1 tablespoon soy sauce
   1 teaspoon sugar
   1 teaspoon vinegar

½ teaspoon salt
a dash of MSG (optional)
1 teaspoon cornstarch, dissolved in
   1 tablespoon water
5 tablespoons vegetable oil

1. Combine pork and Mixture A.
2. Heat 4 tablespoons oil in a hot wok and
   lightly brown the sliced bean curd on both
   sides, remove from wok.
3. Add remaining tablespoon oil and ½ teaspoon salt, stir-fry the green peppers, bamboo
   shoot and mushrooms, cooking each briefly
   before adding next ingredients. Add chili
   peppers and seasoned pork and mix well.
4. When the pork changes color, put the bean
   curd back in. Add Mixture B, and the dash
   of MSG, if desired.
5. Cook for 3 to 4 minutes, stirring constantly.
   Thicken sauce with the dissolved cornstarch.

Tomato and Bean Curd Stew
蕃 茄 豆 腐 *(Fan-ch'ieh-tou-fu)*

This dish has a special tart, fresh flavor and is best when fresh tomatoes are in season.

4 servings
2 blocks bean curd, cut into ½-inch thick
    rectangular pieces
2 tomatoes, dipped in boiling water, peeled
    and cut into 8 wedges
1 green onion, chopped
1 clove garlic, minced
1 tablespoon dried shrimps, soaked in
    3 tablespoons boiling water, drained
    and sprinkled with 1 teaspoon sherry
a pinch of MSG (optional)
1 teaspoon salt
1 teaspoon cornstarch, dissolved in
    1 tablespoon water
2 tablespoons cooked green soybeans
    or green peas.
5 tablespoons vegetable oil

1. Heat 4 tablespoons oil in a hot wok or pan
   and add salt. Fry the tomatoes until they
   break and soften. Add the bean curd, garlic
   and shrimps. Simmer 5 minutes over low
   heat. Add the green onions, MSG and dissolved
   cornstarch.
2. Pour 1 tablespoon oil over the mixture in a
   circular motion.
3. Garnish with soybeans or peas

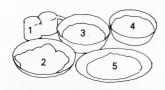

Frozen Bean Curd Stew
砂鍋凍豆腐 *(Sha-kuo-tung-tou-fu)*

This is a fresh tasting stew with many ingredients whose different flavors blend together for a delicious effect.

4 servings

1 block frozen bean curd, rinsed with hot
   water, drained and sliced ¼ -inch thick
6 chicken wings, each cut in half
⅓ bunch any greens, washed
3 medium slices ham, cut into 6 pieces
4 dried Chinese mushrooms, soaked in
   warm water until soft, cut into slices
1 oz. bean threads, soaked in water and
   drained
½ green onion, crushed
1-inch piece fresh ginger, crushed
1 tablespoon shortening
5 cups chicken broth
1 tablespoon Chinese rice wine or sherry
Seasonings:
   2 teaspoons salt
   a pinch of pepper
   a pinch of MSG (optional)

1. Use an earthenware casserole if available. Combine the chicken broth and all other ingredients except greens and seasonings. Bring to a boil and skim off the scum. Reduce heat to low and simmer for about 30 minutes.
2. Heat the shortening in a wok or pan. Stir-fry the greens with a pinch of salt, drain off the liquid, add to the stew. Season with salt, pepper, and MSG. Serve hot.

Pressed Bean Curd Fry
什錦干絲 *(Shih-ching-kan-ssǔ)*

This is a nutritious side dish. It is very colorful and attractive to look at — a good choice for party menus.

4 servings

1 block pressed bean curd, cut into
   thin strips
½ boiled bamboo shoot, cut into thin
   strips
1 carrot, cut into thin strips
½ green pepper, cut into thin strips
5 oz. pork, cut into thin strips
1 oz. pickled mustard green, cut into
   thin strips *(cha-t'sai)*
Mixture A:
   1 tablespoon Chinese rice wine or sherry
   1 tablespoon soy sauce
   1 teaspoon cornstarch
1 tablespoon soy sauce
1½ teaspoons sugar
a pinch of MSG (optional)
4 tablespoons oil

1. Combine the pork and Mixture A.
2. Heat 2 tablespoons oil in a hot wok. Stir-fry pork quickly and remove.
3. Add 2 more tablespoons oil and a dash of salt to the same wok. Stir-fry the bamboo shoots, carrots, green peppers, cha-t'sai, and bean curd, cooking each briefly before adding the next.
4. Add the pork and mix together. Add a little water and season with soy sauce, sugar and MSG. Cook for 3–4 minutes longer.

Pressed Bean Curd and How to Make It   豆腐干 *(Tou-fu-kan)*

In China the people enjoy a wide variety of dishes that include the use of pressed bean curd, called "tou-fu-kan." You may find it in Chinese stores.

To make one block pressed Bean Curd
2 blocks bean curd
1 teaspoon salt

1. Combine bean curd and salt. Stir thoroughly with a wooden spatula, breaking up the blocks of bean curd into little pieces. Heat, continuing to stir, until it comes to a boil.
2. Empty the contents into a strainer which has been lined with several layers of cheesecloth. Wrap neatly and securely. Press between 2 boards and place an additional weight (for example a bowl filled with water) on top. Allow to stand for half a day. (A, B, C, D)
3. Remove hardened bean curd from the cheesecloth. The pressed bean curd is now ready for use as an ingredient for other Chinese dishes. Recipes follow.

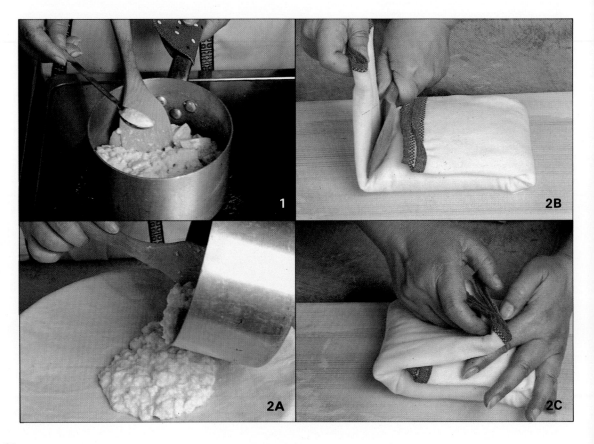

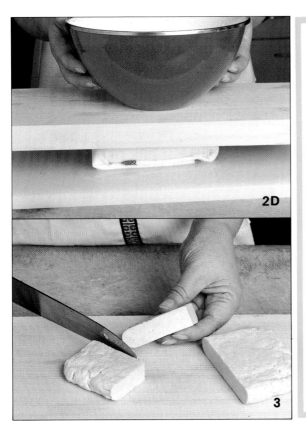

2D

3

Deep-Fried Bean Curd

You can cut bean curd into ½-inch thick slices and deep-fry in vegetable oil.

When bean curd is thus deep-fried, its outer surface becomes crusty and golden brown. Very thin sheets of fried bean curd can be cut into strips and be used in stir-fried dishes. They can also be slit on one edge and carefully opened to form a pocket for a stuffing. Available both fresh and canned, these thin pieces of bean curd are called *"yu-tou-fu"* in Chinese food stores, and *"abura-age"* in Japanese stores. (*"Age"* is pronounced *"ag-eh"*—with short a as in action)

Canned bean curd *(abura-age)* is sold in Japanese food stores.

Stuffed Fried Bean Curd
油豆腐塞肉 *(Yu-tou-fu-sai-jou)*

4 servings

8 pieces deep-fried bean curd (1 can of
  abura-age)
⅔ lb. pork shoulder, ground
5 dried Chinese mushrooms, soaked
  in warm water until soft, drained and
  minced
Mixture A:
  1½ tablespoons soy sauce
  ⅓ teaspoon salt
  a pinch of pepper
  a pinch of MSG (optional)
½ green onion, chopped
1-inch piece fresh ginger, minced
8 toothpicks
Mixture B:
  1 cup water
  1 tablespoon soy sauce
  2 teaspoons sugar
  a pinch of MSG (optional)

1. Pour boiling water over the fried bean curd,
   and squeeze dry. Make a slit along one edge
   and carefully open up the pieces with your
   finger tips, forming a pocket. (In some lo-
   calities, fresh deep-fried bean curd comes in
   10 × 20 sheets. Use only 4 of these. Cut them
   in half and open up from the cut edge.)
2. Combine the ground pork, mushrooms, green
   onion, ginger and Mixture A. Mix thoroughly.
3. Divide the mixture into 8 portions, stuffing
   each of the bean curd pockets. Pinch the
   edges of the openings together. Secure with
   toothpicks.
4. Place the stuffed fried bean curds in a sauce

pan. Add Mixture B. Boil for 5 minutes over
high heat, then reduce heat and simmer for
another 20 minutes. Turn bean curds over
and cook until all liquid dissipated.

Pork and Soybean Sprout Soup
黃豆芽排骨湯
(Huang-tou-ya-p'ai-ku-t'ang)

*This a light soup seasoned with salt and pepper.
If you prefer a heavier flavor, add a bit of soy
sauce when eating.*

4 servings

½ lb. soybean sprouts, roots removed,
  washed and drained
1 lb. pork plate, cut into bite-size pieces
5–6 cups water
1 green onion, crushed
1-inch piece fresh ginger root, crushed
1 tablespoon Chinese rice wine or sherry
2½ teaspoons salt
pepper and MSG (optional) to taste

1. Put the pork, green onion and ginger in a pot,
   adding water. Place over a high heat. Bring
   to a boil and skim off scum.
2. Reduce heat to low and add the wine. Cook
   for 10 minutes, until the water absorbs the
   flavor of the pork.
3. Add the bean sprouts and cook for another
   30–40 minutes, until the bean sprouts and
   the pork become tender. Season with salt,
   MSG and pepper.

Soybean Sprouts and Pickled Mustard Greens

黄豆芽炒鹹菜
(Huang-tou-ya-ch'ao-hsien-t'sai)

4 servings

⅔ lb. soybean sprouts, roots removed, washed and drained
¼ lb. pickled mustard greens, washed, drained and minced
4 tablespoons oil
1½ teaspoons sugar
1 tablespoon soy sauce
a pinch of MSG (optional)

1. Heat 2 tablespoons oil in a wok. Fry the pickled mustard greens, add 1 teaspoon of sugar and transfer to a plate.
2. Add remaining 2 tablespoons of oil to the same wok and stir-fry the bean sprouts quickly over a high heat.
3. Add mustard greens to the bean sprouts and sprinkle with the soy sauce and remainder of sugar, stirring constantly. If there is not enough juice, add a little water. Cover and simmer for 2 to 3 minutes over moderate heat. When the bean sprouts become transparent, transfer to a serving dish. This dish may be served either hot or cold.

Glazed Mung Beans and Dates

綠豆紅棗湯 *(Lü-tou-hung-tsao-t'ang)*

This is a typical Chinese sweet. Served chilled, it is a refreshing dessert on a hot summer's day.

4 servings

1 cup fresh mung beans, washed
20 dried dates, washed
4–5 cups water
4 tablespoons sugar

1. Bring mung beans and water rapidly to a boil over high heat. Then reduce heat to medium and cook for 15 minutes.
2. Add dates, reduce heat still further to low and simmer until dates become large and tender (about 15 minutes). Be careful not to overcook, for the skin of the dates will become broken.
3. Add sugar. If the juice has become too reduced, add a little water. Heat just until sugar is thoroughly melted. Serve hot or cold.

FISH

The Chinese word for fish is pronounced *"yu."* The same pronunciation is given to the word "remain." From this coincidence the Chinese developed a tradition of serving fish at celebrations and happy occasions: the fish *("yu")* served at the meal "guaranteed" that the happiness felt by the participants would remain *("yu")* for a long time.

The Chinese use both fresh- and salt-water fish in their cooking. They prefer fresh-water fish, for these can be kept alive in tubs until the last moment. Many of the kinds used are similar to those available in Western countries: black bass (rockfish), bluefish, carp, cod, flounder, halibut, mullet, perch, pike, plaice (fluke), porgy, seabass, shad, and red snapper. (These are just suggestions, not a complete list. Pick freely among those available in your locality.)

For celebrations and parties the Chinese serve fish whole. A headless, tailless fish is considered incomplete and unaesthetic. There is also a practical reason for leaving the fish intact: fewer juices escape during the cooking process. Choose a fish that weighs 2 lb. or less for cooking whole; a larger fish is too hard to handle.

How to Choose Good Fish

Look for eyes that are bright, not red or soggy. The skin should be glossy.

When you touch the fish, it should feel firm and resilient.

Lesson 5 Fish & Shellfish

▶ Deep-Fried Sweet and Sour Yellow Fish, p. 7

Deep-Fried Sweet-and-Sour Yellow Fish

糖醋黃魚 *(T'ang-t'su-huang-yü)*

Keep the fish whole for this elegant dish. The fish is deep-fried twice for extra crispness.

4 serving
1 yellow fish (2 lb.)
3 dried Chinese mushrooms, soaked in
  water, drained and cut into strips
1 carrot, parboiled and cut into strips
1 small green pepper, cut into strips
½ onion, thinly sliced
2 oz. boiled bamboo shoots, cut into strips
salt and pepper
1 egg yolk, lightly beaten
cornstarch
oil for deep-frying plus 3 tablespoons
  more oil
Sweet-and-Sour Sauce:
  1 tablespoon soy sauce
  3 tablespoons sugar
  3 tablespoons vinegar
  4 tablespoons catchup
  1 tablespoon cornstarch
  1 cup water

1. Clean and scale the fish. Wash well and make 3 or 4 deep slashes along the body.
2. Sprinkle with salt and pepper, brush with egg yolk, and dredge with cornstarch.
3. Heat a generous amount of oil in a wok. Deep-fry the fish slowly, and remove.
4. Still using low heat, deep-fry the vegetables briefly, and remove.
5. Increase the temperature to high, and deep-fry the fish a second time. Remove to a platter and keep warm.
6. Heat 3 tablespoons of oil in a clean wok. Pour in Sauce and stir until it thickens. Add the vegetables, and as soon as they are heated through, pour the sauce over the fish. Serve immediately.

Hearty Yellow Fish Soup
黄 魚 羹 *(Huang-yü-kêng)*

4 servings
¾ lb. yellow fish fillets
1 green onion, thinly sliced
2 tablespoons Chinese rice wine or sherry
1 teaspoon fresh ginger juice
3 cups chicken stock or bouillon
2 slices ham, cut into ½-inch squares
½ block bean curd, cut into ½-inch cubes
5 white mushrooms, thinly sliced
¼ lb. bamboo shoots, cut into ½-inch cubes
Mixture A:
    2 tablespoons Chinese rice wine or sherry
    1 teaspoon salt
    a few grains of pepper
1 tablespoon cornstarch, dissolved in
    2 tablespoons water
1 egg, beaten
a pinch of MSG

1. Place the fish on a heat-proof dish. Add the green onion, and sprinkle with the wine and ginger juice. Steam for 20 minutes. Reserve the juices in the dish. Shred the fish.
2. Place the stock in a saucepan, and add the reserved fish juices. Also add the ham, bean curd, mushrooms and bamboo shoots. Heat, and season with Mixture A.
3. Pour in the dissolved cornstarch. Bring to the boiling point and add the beaten egg. When the soup begins to boil again, add the fish. Season with MSG, and serve hot.

Deep-Fried Fish Sticks
炸 魚 条 *(Cha-yu-t'iao)*

4 servings
½ lb. white fish meat
2 egg whites
Mixture A:
    1 tablespoon flour
    1 tablespoon cornstarch
    a pinch of salt and MSG
oil for deep-frying
1 tomato, thinly sliced
Table Seasonings:
    catchup
    san-chiao-yen

1. Cut the fillet into finger-length pieces and sprinkle with salt and pepper.
2. Beat the egg whites until stiff. Fold in Mixture A. Dip the fish into this coating.
3. Heat the oil in a wok and deep-fry the fish. Place on a serving dish and garnish with the tomato slices. Serve with the table seasonings.

OTHER SEAFOOD

Chinese cooking uses a wide variety of shellfish. Besides such exotic-sounding seafood as ark-shells, razor-shells and shell-ligaments, there are the familiar shrimp, crab, prawns, oysters and scallops. These are deep-fried, stir-fried and braised. Shellfish, like fish, are often deep-fried first and then stir-fried with vegetables; a sauce is added at the last moment. The deep-frying can be done earlier at your convenience to simplify last-minute preparations.

Frozen shellfish should be defrosted in the same way as frozen fish.

Cuttlefish and Squid

There are many varieties of these sea mollusks. In general, cuttlefish has thicker flesh and shorter tentacles than the squid. It also has a large cuttle-bone along the back which is actually an internal shell.

Frozen cuttlefish and squid are cleaned before packaging. Fresh ones can be cleaned at the fish market. To clean squid yourself, remove the skin with knife or scissors, or rub it away under cold running water; remove the ink sac without puncturing it; cut off the tentacles, gelatinous portions and cartilage; wash well. Directions for preparing cuttlefish are given with pictures on page 80.

Cuttlefish and squid have pure white meat and a chewy consistency. The recipes in this chapter call for cuttlefish, but squid can be substituted for it. If neither of these mollusks is available in your area, scallops may be used instead.

Dried Shellfish

China's large size and the necessity for transporting foodstuffs over great distances made the dehydrating of shellfish a practical necessity. Abalone, bêche-de-mer, clams, cuttlefish, jelly-fish, scallops, shrimp and squid—to name just a few!—can be purchased dried, kept indefinitely on your pantry shelf, and used to impart their rich, distinctive flavor to soups and slow-cooked dishes.

Deep-Fried Cuttlefish and Vegetables
炒魷魚什錦 *(Ch'ao-yu-yü-shih-ching)*

4 servings
1 cuttlefish
2 oz. pork, cut into 1 ×2-inch long pieces
Mixture A:
   ½ teaspoon salt
   ½ teaspoon soy sauce
   ½ teaspoon Chinese rice wine or sherry
   a little cornstarch
16 shrimps, shelled and washed in salt water
Mixture B:
   1 tablespoon Chinese rice wine or sherry
   1 tablespoon cornstarch
16 snow peas, strung
2 oz. carrot, cut into strips
2 oz. bamboo shoot, cut into strips
8 small dried Chinese mushrooms, soaked
   in water, drained and cut into thin strips
1 green onion, thinly sliced
Mixture C:
   2 tablespoons soy sauce
   1 tablespoon Chinese rice wine or sherry
   a pinch of sugar, salt, pepper and MSG
oil for deep-frying plus 2 tablespoons
   more oil

1. Clean and score the cuttlefish as in the previous recipe. Slice into 1 × 1½-inch pieces.
2. Coat the pork with Mixture A.
3. Coat the shrimps with Mixture B.
4. Heat the oil in a wok and deep-fry the snow peas quickly. Then deep-fry the pork, the shrimp, and the carrots, mushrooms and bamboo shoot. Drain everything.

5. Heat the 2 tablespoons of oil in a clean wok, and stir-fry the green onion. Add the deep-fried vegetables except snow peas, and stir-fry briefly. Add and stir-fry the cuttlefish, pork and shrimps. Pour in Mixture C.
6. Place on a serving dish and garnish with the snow peas.

Deep-Fried Prawns
軟炸明蝦 *(Juan-cha-ming-hsia)*

4 servings
12 prawns, shelled and deveined
   (but leave tail-shell on)
1 teaspoon salt
1 tablespoon Chinese rice wine or sherry
½ teaspoon salt
Batter:
   1 egg, beaten
   3 tablespoons flour
   ¼ teaspoon salt
   ⅓ teaspoon baking powder
oil for deep-frying
several lettuce leaves for garnish
Table seasonings:
   san-chiao-yen or catchup

1. Rub the prawns with salt, then wash and drain. Sprinkle with the wine and the ½ teaspoon salt. Set aside while preparing the batter.
2. Mix all the ingredients to make batter.
3. Heat the oil in a wok. Dip the prawns in the batter, and deep-fry them until they become light golden brown.
4. Serve on a bed of lettuce leaves with the table seasonings.

Fried Shrimps
油爆蝦 *(Yu-pao-hsia)*

4 servings
⅔ lb. shrimps
1 tablespoon soy sauce
½ tablespoon Chinese rice wine or sherry
2 tablespoons minced green onion
1 tablespoon minced fresh ginger
1 teaspoon sugar
a pinch of salt
oil for deep-frying, plus 3 more
   tablespoons oil

1. Remove the heads of the shrimps, but leave the shells intact, devein and wash. Sprinkle with the soy sauce and wine.
2. Deep-fry the shrimps in heated oil. Remove and drain.
3. Heat the 3 tablespoons of oil in a clean wok and stir-fry the minced green onion and ginger. Mix in the shrimps. Add the sugar and salt, mix thoroughly, and serve.

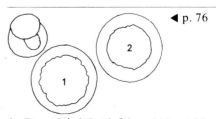

◀ p. 76

1. Deep-Fried Cuttlefish and Vegetables, p. 78
2. Fried Shrimps, p. 79

Deep-Fried Cuttlefish, Szechwan Style

魚香魷花 *(Yü-hsiang-yu-hua)*

4 servings

1¼ lb. cuttlefish
1 green pepper, cut into 1 × 2-inch pieces
½ green onion, cut into 1½ -inch long
   matchsticks
1-inch piece fresh ginger, cut into strips
1 clove garlic, cut into strips
2 chili peppers, cut into strips
Mixture A:
   1½ teaspoons soy sauce
   1 tablespoon Chinese rice wine or sherry
   ½ teaspoon salt
   a little pepper and MSG (optional)
2 teaspoons cornstarch, dissolved in
   1 tablespoon water
oil for deep-frying

1. Slice open the cuttlefish, and peel off the 4
   layers of skin.
2. Place the cuttlefish on a cutting board, opened
   out flat with the outside surface on top.
   Score it diagonally, cutting about ⅔ of the
   way through the flesh. Score the cuttlefish in
   the opposite direction so that you have a
   pattern of squares about 1-inch in size. (A, B)
3. Cut the cuttlefish into 1 × 2-inch pieces. Pat
   dry.
4. Heat the oil to 300°F. Add the cuttlefish all
   at once and deep-fry quickly. (If you add the
   pieces little by little, the first ones will be
   scorched.)
5. As the cuttlefish becomes cooked, the scoring
   marks will become distinct. When this
   happens, remove and drain.
6. Leave 2 tablespoons of oil in the wok. Stir-
   fry the garlic, ginger, chili peppers and green
   onion. Then add and stir-fry the green pepper.
   Add the cuttlefish, and mix everything together well. Stir in Mixture A. Pour in the
   dissolved cornstarch, using a circular motion,
   and heat just until thickened.

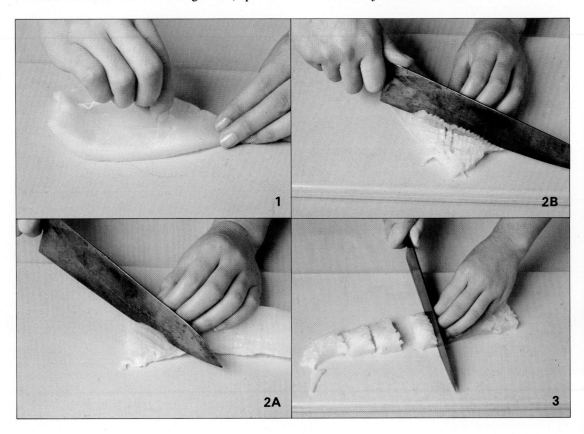

Deep-Fried Oysters
炸生蠔 *(Cha-sheng-hao)*

*East and West meet in the deep-fried oyster:
Chinese and Western cooks prepare this dish in
very similar ways.*

4 servings
½ lb. shucked oysters
1 tablespoon Chinese rice wine or sherry
a little salt and pepper
⅓ cup flour
1 egg, beaten
bread crumbs
oil for deep-frying
several parsley sprigs for garnish
Table seasonings:
    san-chiao-yen or catchup

1. Wash the oysters in a bowlful of salted water
   (3 tablespoons salt). Then wash in fresh
   water. Drain.
2. Sprinkle with the wine, salt and pepper.
3. Dredge with flour, dip them in the egg, and
   coat with bread crumbs.
4. Heat the oil and deep-fry the oysters.
5. Garnish the serving dish with the parsley,
   and serve with catchup and *san-chiao-yen*.

Scrambled Eggs with Oysters
蠣蝗炒蛋 *(Li-huang-ch'ao-tan)*

4 servings
15 oysters, shucked, washed and drained
2 green onions, cut into ½-inch lengths
4 eggs
½ teaspoon salt
a little pepper and MSG (optional)
3 tablespoons oil

1. Beat the eggs, lightly adding the green onion,
   salt, pepper and MSG. Stir in the oysters.
2. Heat the oil in a wok and pour in the mixture. Stirring continuously, cook until the
   eggs are softly done. Do not overcook.

Stir-Fried Scallops with Chili Peppers
魚香鮮貝 *(Yü-hsiang-hsien-pei)*

Use either fresh or frozen scallops for this dish.

4 servings
10 scallops, cut in half, washed in
    salt water and drained
½ lb. bamboo shoots, cut into thin strips
1 green pepper, cut into thin strips
4 dried Chinese mushrooms, soaked in
    water, drained and cut into thin strips
1 green onion, cut into thin strips
1-inch piece fresh ginger, minced
1 clove garlic, minced
2 chili peppers, chopped
Mixture A:
    1 tablespoon soy sauce
    1 tablespoon Chinese rice wine or sherry
    1 teaspoon sugar
a pinch of salt
2 teaspoons cornstarch, dissolved in
    1 tablespoon water
5 tablespoons oil

1. Heat 2 tablespoons of the oil in a hot wok,
   and add the salt. Stir-fry the green peppers,
   bamboo shoots and mushroom. Remove.
2. Heat the remaining 3 tablespoons of oil.
   Stir-fry the green onion, ginger, garlic and
   chili peppers. Add the scallops and stir-fry
   briefly. Return the cooked vegetables to
   the wok. Add Mixture A, and toss together.
   Pour in the dissolved cornstarch mixture,
   using a circular motion.

Dried Scallops with Chinese Cabbage
干貝燒白菜 *(Kan-pei-shao-pai-t'sai)*

A good flavor-combination.

4 servings
2 dried scallops
½ cup boiling water
1⅓ lb. Chinese cabbage, cut into
    1 × 4-inch strips
½ cup soup stock
2 tablespoons soy sauce
1 teaspoon sugar
2 teaspoons cornstarch, dissolved in
    2 teaspoons cold water
4 tablespoons oil
a few drops of sesame oil

1. Pour the boiling water over the scallops and
   let soak until soft.
2. Heat the oil in a wok, and stir-fry the scallops
   and Chinese cabbage. Add the stock, the
   scallop-flavored water, soy sauce and sugar.
   (If using bouillon cubes rather than home-
   made stock, you may need less soy sauce.)
   Bring to a boil, then turn down heat and
   simmer about 10 minutes.
3. Just before the liquid has completely evapo-
   rated, pour in the dissolved cornstarch. Cook
   until thickened. At the last minute, sprinkle
   with a few drops of sesame oil. Mix and serve
   immediately.

Westerners generally go to a Chinese restaurant for a regular meal at noon or night, and so the concept of Chinese snacks is probably an unfamiliar one. Chinese snacks are very closely connected with the people's way of thinking about food and with the tea-drinking habits of the country. A word of explanation about these will help you understand why all the recipes in this chapter are considered snacks.

The Chinese divide their foods into two general categories: *t'sai* and *tien-hsin*. *T'sai* refers to the appetizers that are served with wine and to the dishes that are served with rice. All stir-fried, stewed, steamed dishes, even soup for example, are *t'sai*. In contrast to Western-style meals, these dishes are considered to be accompaniments to rice, not the other way around.

Everything that is not *t'sai* is called *tien-hsin*.

The noodle dishes, dumplings, buns and cookies that you will learn to make in this chapter are all *tien-hsin*. These foods are served at mealtime, sometimes as side dishes or dessert and other times as a main dish in a light meal. The Chinese also eat them as snacks in homes and teahouses, while talking with friends and drinking innumerable cups of tea.

In a typical teahouse in the Canton region, waiters thread their way between the crowded tables carrying snacks on large trays or in wagons. They stop at each table, and the customer picks out the food he likes. Later he will pay according to the number of dishes at his place.

When you serve *tien-hsin* at tea-time, you might like to accompany the food with tea fixed as the Chinese do.

Lesson *6*
Snacks & Cakes

▶ Bean Jam Buns, p. 87
▶ Four-Colored *Shao-mai*, p. 87

HOW TO MAKE CHINESE TEA

A Chinese teacup has a lid and no handle. Put about 1 teaspoon of tea into each cup, pour in boiling water and cover. After 3 or 4 minutes the tea leaves will sink to the bottom, and tea is ready to drink. Slide the lid back a little but do not entirely remove it when drinking. When the cup is empty, take off the lid and pour in boiling water again. Tea leaves can be used about 3 times. The second infusion is considered to be the most delicious.

DUMPLINGS AND SPRING ROLLS

These delicate filled pastries can be served as appetizers or as a side dish. The dumplings, when served in larger quantities, can be the main dish in a light meal.

Dumplings are smaller than spring rolls. *Shao-mai* are cylindrical and have open tops. *Chiao-tzu* are half-moon shaped and are sealed tightly.

The pastry base for these delicacies is called a "skin." Skins may be purchased in Chinese grocery stores, but they are much more delicious when made at home. Both the ready-made and home-made skins will keep for 3 or 4 days in the refrigerator, and for several months in the freezer. Defrost them completely before using.

NOODLES

Chinese noodles are made with eggs which give them a yellowish cast. Choose noodles which are light in color; dark ones have been artificially colored and should be avoided.

You may buy both dried and fresh noodles in Chinese grocery stores. The dried ones come in 3 × 5-inch packages and will keep indefinitely on your pantry shelf. The fresh ones, which require only parboiling or steeping in boiling water, should be refrigerated and used within a few days. They may also be frozen.

HOW TO COOK DRIED NOODLES

Bring water to a boil and add the noodles. Cook over high heat, loosening the noodles with chopsticks or a fork. When the boiling water starts to rise, add a little cold water. This prevents it from boiling over and also improves the taste. The noodles are done when they become transparent.

STEAMED BUNS

Buns are very highly valued by the Chinese. Traditionally they have been offered to the gods to pacify them and cause them to look with favor on the people. Originally, buns contained no stuffing. But today, the Chinese place bean jam, sausage, sesame seeds or red dates, etc., inside the buns. Sometimes the buns are deep-fried as well as steamed.

COOKIES

There are called "dry desserts" by the Chinese. Like Western cookies, they will keep for a long time in tightly closed containers and, if you can hide them from the family, are handy to have when guests drop in unexpectedly.

Four-Colored *Shao-mai*
四喜烧壳 *(Ssu-hsi-shao-mai)*

The top of the shao-mai *is divided into four parts, into which are put ingredients of different colors.*

30 *shao-mai*
30 *shao-mai* skins, see page 92
Filling:
   1 lb. ground pork
Mixture A:
   2 teaspoons sesame oil
   2 teaspoons Chinese rice wine or sherry
   3 tablespoons soy sauce
   ½ teaspoon salt / 1 teaspoon sugar
   a few grains of pepper
"Four-colors":
   2 ham slices, minced
   1 bunch of spinach, boiled and minced
   2 hard-boiled egg yolks, sieved
   2 dried Chinese mushrooms, soaked
     in water and drained
   1 tablespoon soy sauce
   a pinch of sugar

1. Thoroughly combine the ground pork and Mixture A. Make 30 little balls of the meat, and place one in the center of each skin. Pinch the edges together as shown in the photo, forming a 4-leaf clover.
2. Cook the Chinese mushrooms in the soy sauce and sugar for about 5 minutes. Mince.
3. Place a bit of ham in one of the openings of the 4-leaf clover. Do the same with the spinach, mushrooms and egg yolk, thus forming the 4 colors.
4. Oil the bottom of the steamer rack, and set the *shao-mai* on it. Cover and steam for 7 or 8 minutes over high heat.

Bean Jam Buns
豆沙包子 *(Tou-sha-pao-tzu)*

Bean jam is red-bean paste, thick and sweet, available in cans in Oriental specialty shops. This is a pink-tinted bun that is shaped like a peach.

10 buns
Dough:
   same as for Soft Meat Buns, see page 91
Filling:
   ½ lb. bean jam
   2½ tablespoons lard
   a pinch of salt
a little food coloring (green and red)
10 pieces wax paper (2-inch squares)

1. To prepare the dough, follow steps 1–3 in the recipe for Soft Meat Buns. However, before rolling the dough into circles, take out a little and save it for decorating the buns.
2. Put the ingredients for the filling in a small pan and mix them together over low heat. Let cook, then roll the filling into 10 balls. Place them on the circles of dough, and wrap the dough around them.
3. With the sealed side down, make a line up the middle of the bun and pinch the top to give it the shape of a peach.
4. Mix the green food coloring with the reserved dough. Roll it out and cut it into 20 leaves. Place 2 leaves on each bun.
5. Place the buns on the wax-paper squares set in the steamer rack, and let sit for 8 minutes. Then steam for 8 minutes over high heat.
6. Dilute the red food coloring and brush it on the buns, giving them a peach-like color.

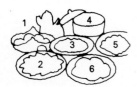

Ham and Chicken in Noodle Soup
鶏火湯麺 (*Chi-huo-t'ang-mien*)

4 servings

4 packages of dried Chinese egg noodles
¼ lb. chicken wings
6 slices ham, cut into thin strips 2-inch long
12 fresh snow peas, strung and parboiled in salt water; cut into thin strips
2-inch piece green onion, chopped finely
8 cups chicken stock (see page 43.)
1–2 teaspoons Chinese rice wine or sherry
a little of salt and pepper

1. Sprinkle the chicken wings with the wine, salt and pepper. Steam for 20 minutes. Cut the meat into thin strips, or tear it into shreds with your hands.
2. Heat the stock, and season with salt and pepper.
3. Cook the noodles in a generous amount of water. Drain, and place in a warmed tureen or individual deep soup bowls. Pour the hot soup over the noodles. Arrange the chicken, ham and snow peas on top, and sprinkle with the green onion.

Soft-Fried Noodles
炒軟麺 (*Ch'ao-juan-mien*)

4 servings

4 packages dried Chinese egg noodles
¼ lb. pork, cut into thin strips
Mixture A:
   1 tablespoon soy sauce
   1 tablespoon Chinese rice wine or sherry
   1 teaspoon cornstarch
6 cabbage leaves, cored and the remainder cut into thin strips
2–3 stalks spinach, cut into 2-inch lengths
Mixture B:
   2 tablespoons soy sauce
   2 teaspoons sugar
   1½ teaspoons salt
   5 tablespoons water
6 tablespoons oil
a little salt and salad oil for noodles

1. Combine pork and Mixture A. Let sit for 15 minutes.
2. Cook the noodles in a generous amount of water. Drain, and sprinkle with salt and salad oil while still hot.
3. Heat 2 tablespoons of the oil in a wok. Stir-fry the pork, and remove when it changes color.
4. Add 4 tablespoons oil to the wok and stir-fry the noodles briefly. Add the vegetables, and stir-fry until they are done. Then mix in the pork. Pour in Mixture B, and stir-fry until thoroughly heated.

Spring Rolls
春 捲 (Ch'un-chüan)

4 servings
8 spring roll skins
2 oz. thinly sliced pork, cut into thin strips
Mixture A:
    1 teaspoon Chinese rice wine or sherry
    1 teaspoon soy sauce and cornstarch
    a few grains of pepper
2 dried large Chinese mushrooms, soaked
    in water and drained. Cut into strips.
2½ oz. boiled bamboo shoots, cut into strips
2 cabbage leaves, cut into strips
½ teaspoon salt
flour-and-water paste
oil for deep-frying plus 3 tablespoons
    more oil
Table seasonings: see page 34.

1. Combine the pork and Mixture A. Let sit for 15 minutes.
2. Heat 3 tablespoons of the oil in a wok, and stir-fry the pork briefly. Remove.
3. Heat the remaining 1 tablespoon oil and add the salt. Stir-fry the vegetables, then mix in the pork. Turn off the heat and let the filling cool thoroughly.
4. Place some of the filling a little above the center of each spring roll skin. Fold the upper edge over the filling, turn in the 2 sides, and roll it down to the bottom. Brush the bottom edge with the flour-and-water paste to seal it thoroughly.
5. Heat the deep-frying oil over moderate heat. Deep-fry the spring rolls until golden. Turn them frequently.
6. Serve immediately with table seasonings.

Soft Meat Buns
肉 包 子 (Jou-pao-tzu)

10 Buns
Pastry:
    4 tablespoons bread flour or semolina
    1½ cups all-purpose flour
    1 tablespoon dry yeast
    2 tablespoons lard or shortening
    3 tablespoons sugar
    ½ cup warm (85° F.) water
Filling:
    1 lb. ground pork
Mixture A:
    2 tablespoons sesame oil
    2 tablespoons Chinese rice wine or sherry
    2 tablespoons soy sauce
    1 teaspoon sugar / 1½ teaspoons salt
    a few grains of pepper
10 pieces wax paper (1-inch squares)

1. Sift the bread flour and all-purpose flour into a bowl. Using another bowl, pour in the warm water. Add the yeast, lard and sugar, and mix well. Combine the yeast mixture and flour. Knead well with the hands. Cover with a damp cloth, and let sit in a warm place until it doubles in size (about 30 minutes).
2. Knead the dough again until it becomes elastic. Divide into 10 pieces, and roll into circles 4 or 5 inches in diameter.
3. Combine the ground pork and Mixture A. Divide into 10 balls. Place a meat ball on each circle of dough. Fold the dough around it and pinch the center to seal it well.
4. Place the buns on the wax-paper squares. Set in the steamer rack, and let sit for about 15 minutes. Then steam for 12 or 15 minutes over high heat.

How to Make Skins for *Shao-mai* and *Chiao-tzu*

This recipe makes 30 shao-mai *skins (about 3-inches in diameter) and 20* chiao-tzu *skins (3½-4-inches). Flour with a high gluten content, the same kind that is used for making Italian pasta, gives a much more satisfactory result than regular all-purpose flour.*

2 cups bread flour or semolina
1 cup boiling water
flour for dusting the board

1. Slowly add the boiling water to the bread flour, stirring constantly with chopsticks or a fork.
2. When it is cool enough to handle, knead it well. Transfer the dough to a floured board, and continue to knead until it feels elastic and has a "give."
3. Cover it with a damp cloth, and put aside for 30 minutes.
4. Transfer the dough to a floured board, and roll it with your hands into a long stick.
5. Cut the dough into chunks—30 pieces for *shao-mai,* 20 pieces for *chiao-tzu.*
6. Press the pieces into a flat, round shape with the heel of your hand.

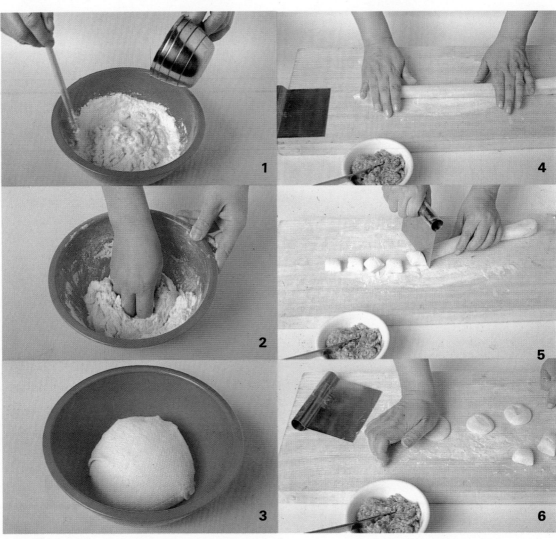

How to Wrap *Shao-mai*

A. Roll out the pieces still thinner.
B. Hold the skin in your cupped hand, and place the filling in the center with a knife.
C. Flatten the top with the knife, and the bottom by pressing it against the board.

How to Wrap *Chiao-tzu*

A. Roll out the pieces, keeping the center a little thicker than the edges.
B. Keeping your hand flat, hold the skin. Place the filling in the center. The finished shape will be better if the filling is spread in an oblong shape.
C. Dampen the edges, and fold them together. Seal the edges firmly by pinching them.

In some areas, purchased skins will be square rather than round, but the wrapping instructions, no matter what the shape of the skin, are the same.

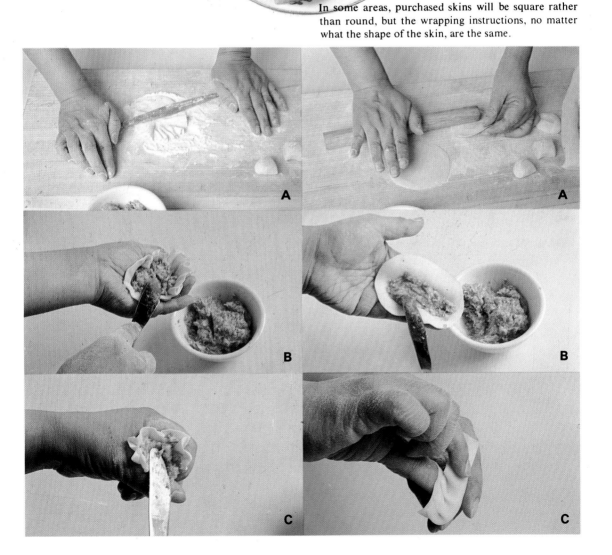

Fried *Chiao-tzu*
鍋 貼 餃 子 *(Kuo-t'ieh-chiao-tzu)*

20 *Chiao-tzu*
20 *chiao-tzu* skins, see p. 92
Filling:
  1 lb. ground pork
Mixture A:
  1 tablespoon Chinese rice wine or sherry
  1 tablespoon sesame oil
  3 tablespoons soy sauce
  2 teaspoons sugar
  1 teaspoon salt
6 Chinese cabbage leaves, boiled,
  drained and minced
2 tablespoons oil
3 tablespoons water
Table seasonings:
  Vinegar and soy sauce mixed together
  Mustard and soy sauce mixed together
  la-yu

1. Combine the ground pork and Mixture A. Let sit for 30 minutes. Add the minced Chinese cabbage, and mix well. Add a little water. Stuff the *chiao-tzu* skins (see page 92).
2. Heat the oil and place *chiao-tzu* in a frying pan. Fry until the bottom becomes a little browned. Pour in enough water to come halfway up the *chiao-tzu*. Cover and cook over moderate heat until no liquid is left. It is not necessary to turn the *chiao-tzu*.
3. Cover the frying pan with a plate and turn the pan over so that the browned side of the *chiao-tzu* faces upwards. Serve hot with the table seasonings.

Boiled *Chiao-tzu*
紅 油 水 餃 *(Hung-yu-shui-chiao)*

These are eaten with a sesame-flavored sauce. For a variation, you can serve boiled chiao-tzu *(without the sesame sauce) in s bowl of chicken consommé.*

20 *Chiao-tzu*
Chiao-tzu skins, see p. 92
Filling:
1 lb. ground pork
Mixture A:
  1 tablespoon Chinese rice wine or sherry
  1 tablespoon sesame oil
  3 tablespoons soy sauce
  2 teaspoons sugar
6 Chinese cabbage leaves, boiled, drained and minced
Mixture B:
  ½ teaspoon minced garlic
  1½ tablespoons soy sauce
  1 tablespoon sesame seeds, pulverized
  1 teaspoon sesame oil / 1 teaspoon vinegar
  ½ teaspoon sugar / ½ teaspoon *la-yu*
  a pinch of MSG (optional)

1. Combine the ingredients in Mixture B, and set aside.
2. Mix together the ground pork and Mixture A. Add the minced Chinese cabbage and mix well. Stuff the skins with the meat mixture and seal (see p. 93.)
3. Cook the *chiao-tzu* in a generous amount of boiling water. When the water returns to the boil, pour in some cold water. When the water boils up a second time, remove the *chiao-tzu* and drain them.
4. Pour Mixture B over the hot *chiao-tzu*, and serve immediately.

Almond Cookies
杏仁酥 *(Hsing-jen-su)*

These are wonderfully crispy.

24 cookies

⅔ cup lard or shortening
1⅔ cups sugar
½ teaspoon almond extract
4 cups all-purpose flour, sifted well
2 teaspoons baking powder
½ teaspoon baking soda
1 egg yolk, beaten
24 almonds

Preheat oven to 375°F.

1. Beat the lard well with a whip or electric mixer. Add the sugar and almond extract and beat further until it becomes creamy.
2. Mix the flour to the lard little by little. Add the baking powder and baking soda and knead well. Then divide into 24 balls.
3. Flatten the balls into ¼-inch thick rounds. Brush the egg yolk over the surface.
4. Put an almond on each cookie and press it in with your finger.
5. Place on a cookie sheet and bake in the preheated oven for about 15 minutes.

Deep-Fried Cookies
開口笑 *(K'ai-K'ou-hsiao)*

The Chinese name literally means "laughing faces," which, as you can see, these cookies actually resemble.

20 balls

2 cups all-purpose flour
2 teaspoons baking powder
1½ tablespoons lard or shortening
1 cup sugar
1 egg
⅔ cup water
1 cup white sesame seeds
little flour for dusting
oil for deep-frying

1. Sift together the flour and baking powder.
2. Whip the lard and add the sugar and egg. Then, add the flour and baking powder, and mix well.
3. Pour in the water little by little, using only enough to make the dough resilient.
4. Transfer the dough to a floured board and roll it into a stick with your hands. Divide into balls. Coat them with white sesame seeds.
5. Bring the oil to a high temperature over strong heat, then reduce heat to low. Deep-fry the balls until they become golden brown and cracks form on the surface.

Five
Kinds
of
Chiao-tzu

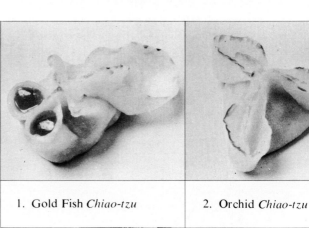

1. Gold Fish *Chiao-tzu*   2. Orchid *Chiao-tzu*

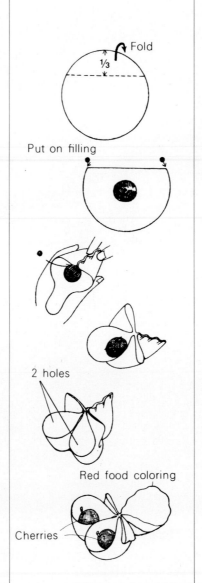

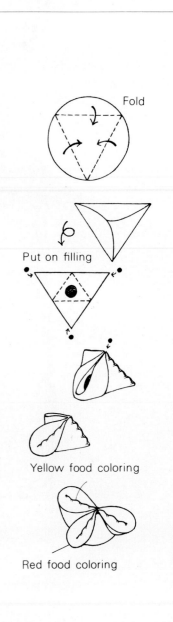

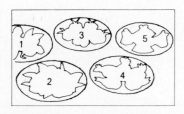

◄See pp. 96, 97
1. Gold Fish *Chiao-tzu*
2. Orchid *Chiao-tzu*
3. Butterfry *Chiao-tzu*
4. Phoenix *Chiao-tzu*
5. Frog *Chiao-tzu*

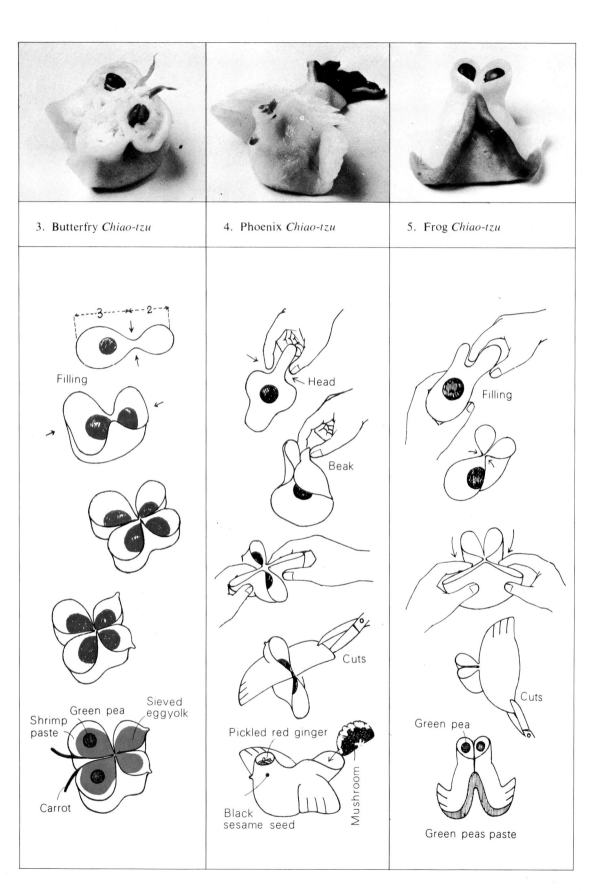

3. Butterfry *Chiao-tzu*   4. Phoenix *Chiao-tzu*   5. Frog *Chiao-tzu*

Filling

Sieved
eggyolk
Green pea
Shrimp
paste

Carrot

Head

Beak

Cuts

Pickled red ginger

Black
sesame seed

Mushroom

Filling

Cuts

Green pea

Green peas paste

Five Kinds of *Shao-mai*

1. Glutinous Rice *Shao-mai*
2. Cicada *Shao-mai*
3. Four Colored *Shao-mai*
4. Bean Jam *Shao-mai*
5. Crabmeat *Shao-mai*

▶ See p. 102

Five Kinds of *Shao-mai*

Cicada *Shao-mai*

20 *shao-mai* skins, see page 92
Filling:
  ½ lb. bean jam
40 green peas

Stuff the skins with the bean jam and garnish with green peas. Steam for 7–8 minutes over high heat.

Bean Jam *Shao-mai*

18 *shao-mai* skins, see page 92
Filling:
  ½ lb. bean jam
cherries and angelica, minced
hard-boiled egg yolk, sieved

Stuff the skins with the bean jam. Place cherries, angelica, and eggyolk on the top of *shao-mai*.

Four-Colored *Shao-mai*
See page 87.

Glutinous Rice *Shao-mai*

20 *shao-mai* skins, see page 92
2 cups glutinous rice, washed and soaked overnight.
2 slices ham, minced
4 tablespoons boiled bamboo shoot, minced
2 Chinese mushrooms, soaked in water, drained and
  minced

Place rice in a bowl. Add 2 cups of water and steam for 40–50 minutes. Sauté ham, bamboo shoot and mushroom with oil. Add 2 tablespoons soy sauce, 1 teaspoon sugar, salt and pepper. Add rice and mix. Fill and press mixture into *shao-mai*. Steam for 7–8 minutes over high heat.

Steamed Buns
花 捲 *(Hua-chuan)*

In China these buns have no stuffing and may be eaten with shredded chicken or other meat. They are often shaped likes butterflies.

10 Butterfly Buns
4 tablespoons bread flour or semolina
1½ cups all-purpose flour
1 tablespoon dry yeast
2 tablespoons lard or shortening
3 tablespoons sugar
½ cup warm (85° F.) water
oil for dough
red food coloring
wax paper

1. Sift the bread flour and all-purpose flour into a bowl. Pour the warm water into another bowl and add the yeast, lard and sugar. Mix well.
2. Knead well with the hands. Then cover with a damp cloth and let sit for about 30 minutes in a warm place.
3. Roll the dough into a long stick and cut it into 1-inch pieces. Press them into round shapes with your hands, then roll them into 2½-inches circles.
4. Brush oil thinly on one side. Fold in half, with the oiled surface on the inside. Make little notches on the rounded edge for the butterfly wings (picture C). Pull out the head with your fingers. Draw lines on the body with a spatula (picture D).
5. Place on a sheet of wax paper. Set on the steamer rack and leave for 7 or 8 minutes, then steam over high heat for about 6 minutes.
6. Make the eyes with several drops of red food coloring (picture E).

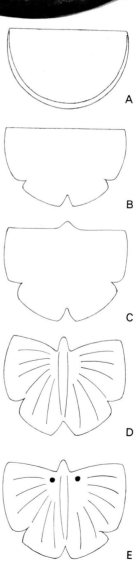

A

B

C

D

E

CHINESE DINNER PARTIES

In China, an invitation to dinner is the best expression of friendship that can be offered. Though party dishes can be very, very eleborate (and we include some in this chapter), you may also serve everyday dishes. The important point is that they be prepared and served from the heart.

The food is placed on large platters in the center of the table, and each guest helps himself. This way of serving food creates a relaxed and friendly atmosphere.

The Menu

A dinner party usually consists of three parts: hors d'oeuvre, main dishes and dessert. The total number of dishes is often eight to ten, with many of the dishes partially or fully prepared in advance.

Hors d'Oeuvres: These are served chilled or at room temperature. The usual number is 4, but with guests who are light drinkers, 3 should be sufficient. For guests who like to drink, keep the hors d'oeuvres strong flavored, and serve rather lightly seasoned main dishes.

Main Dishes: There is a standard order for bringing main dishes to the table. First serve deep-fried foods, then stir-fried foods, then boiled or steamed dishes, and finally foods with sauces.

Soup and rice follow these dishes: The number of main dishes will vary according to the number of guests and the formality of the occasion. It is the Chinese custom to serve an even number of dishes.

Desserts: Because Chinese cooking uses a great deal of spicy seasonings such as garlic, ginger and soy sauce, sweet desserts are usually served at the end of the meal. However, there are no hard and fast rules, and if you prefer, you may serve *shao-mai*, spring rolls, and some of the other dishes included in the chapter on snacks.

Variety is at the heart of Chinese cooking and should be taken into consideration when planning your menu. Variety can be achieved by using different cooking techniques (do not make everything deep-fried), different ingredients (one shrimp dish at a meal is enough) and different temperatures (serve hot and cold dishes together).

Lesson 7 Entertainment

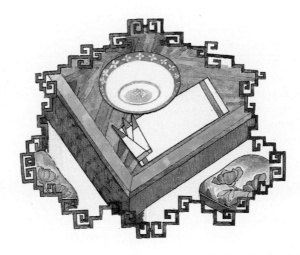

▶ Firepot, p. 10

Firepot   什錦火鍋 *(Shih-ching-huo-kuo)*

A very festive meal-in-a-dish for cozy winter entertaining. A pot of simmering, mixed ingredients is placed in the center of the table. Each person removes his own food with chopsticks (or fondue forks) and dips it into a bowl of sauce. As the finale, dilute the dipping sauce with the marvelously flavored soup and drink up! If you do not have a firepot (see p. 11 for description), you may use an electric chafing dish or deep skillet, an earthenware casserole or even a soup pot placed over a hotplate to keep it warm at the table.

4 servings
1 lb. chicken backs and necks
¼ lb. ground pork
Seasonings A:
   a dash of salt and pepper
   1 teaspoon minced green onion
⅓ lb. boneless chicken
Seasonings B:
   a dash of salt and pepper
   1 teaspoon Chinese rice wine or sherry
5 dried Chinese mushrooms, soaked in
   hot water and drained
1 tablespoon soy sauce
8 shrimps, shelled
½ Chinese cabbage
¼ ib. roast pork, thinly sliced
2 canned abalone, thinly sliced
1 oz. bean threads, soaked in hot water
   and drained
6 quail's eggs, hard-boiled
1 head lettuce
Dipping Sauce:
   mixture of equal parts vinegar and
    soy sauce

1. Prepare the chicken soup stock before the day when you serve this recipe. Bring 10 cups of water to a boil and add the chicken backs and necks. Skim off scum. Continue to boil over moderate heat until the soup is reduced to half.

2. Mix the ground pork with Seasonings A and form into 1-inch balls. Steam for 15 minutes over strong heat.

3. Mix the chicken wings with Seasonings B, and steam for 15 minutes over high heat. Cut into thin slices.

4. Sprinkle the softened mushrooms with the soy sauce, and steam for 15 minutes over medium heat.

5. Parboil the shrimps and Chinese cabbage separately. Use salt water for the shrimps. Cut the Chinese cabbage into oblong pieces.

6. To assemble the fire pot, make a bed of the Chinese cabbage and arrange all the other ingredients, except for the eggs and lettuce, on top. Put the eggs and lettuce at the borders of each ingredient. Heat the chicken stock and pour it over everything.

7. Cooking procedure: If using a fire pot, ignite the charcoal and place it in the chimney before arranging the ingredients. When the soup returns to the boil the diners may eat. If using an electric chafing dish, bring to a boil over strong heat, then lower the temperature control to maintain a simmer. If using an electric hotplate, bring the casserole to a boil on the kitchen stove.

8. Give each person a small bowl for the dipping sauce.

A very beautiful hors d'oeuvre, and not too difficult if you prepare ahead; the day before the party, soak the jellyfish and prepare steps 2 and 3; early the next day, marinate the jellyfish; several hours before the party begins, arrange the food on the platter, cover with plastic wrap, and refrigerate or set in a cool place.

4 servings

⅓ lb. dried jellyfish, passed through
   boiling water and soaked overnight
   in cold water
Mixture A:
   1 teaspoon Chinese rice wine or sherry
   1 teaspoon soy sauce
   1 teaspoon vinegar
   1 teaspoon sesame oil
   1 teaspoon sugar
⅓ lb. chicken wings
Mixture B:
   2-inches green onion
   1-inch piece fresh ginger
   1 teaspoon Chinese rice wine or sherry
   a little salt and pepper
12 shrimps, shells left on, washed in
   salted water and drained
oil for deep-frying
Mixture C:
   2 cups water
   ½ tablespoon sugar
   1 tablespoon Chinese rice wine or sherry
   ½ teaspoon salt
   a pinch of MSG (optional)
1 canned abalone, thinly sliced
¼ lb. cheese, thinly sliced
¼ lb. ham slices, thinly sliced
¼ lb. roast pork*, thinly sliced

1 cucumber, thinly sliced
1 tomato, thinly sliced
6 stalks canned asparagus, cut in half
7 cherries
6 sprigs parsley

*See recipe for roast pork on page 41. You can also use pork barbecued with honey and spices that is available at Chinese grocery stores.

1. Shred the jellyfish, wash and drain, and mix with Mixture A.
2. Place the chicken wings on a heatproof dish. Place the green onion and ginger on top, and sprinkle with the wine, salt and pepper. Steam for about 15 minutes. Cool, and cut at the joint.
3. To prepare the shrimps, heat the oil and deep-fry the shrimps briefly. Combine the rest of the ingredients and Mixture C in a sauce-pan. Add the shrimps and bring them rapidly to a boil over strong heat. Turn off the heat as soon as they have boiled and let cool in the liquid.
4. Arrange the ingredients on a large serving dish, as shown in the picture. Garnish with cherries and parsley.

See p. 108 ▶

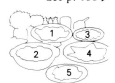

Almond Jelly

See p. 55

Shrimp Toast

蝦仁吐司 *(Hsia-jen-t'u-ssu)*

4 servings
½ lb. shrimps
10 oz. pork fat, finely minced
Mixture A:
　　1 egg
　　1 teaspoon juice from fresh ginger
　　½ teaspoon salt
　　2 teaspoons Chinese rice wine or sherry
　　1 tablespoon cornstarch
5 slices bread
5 walnuts, coarsely broken
minced parsley
oil for deep-frying

1. Shell and devein the shrimps. Pat dry and mince finely. Crush the shrimps and the pork fat with a pestle or the back of a spoon. Combine with Mixture A.
2. Cut the bread into "bamboo leaves," as shown in the pictures. Spread one side with the shrimp mixture, and sprinkle with the parsley and walnuts.
3. Steam for 3 minutes.
4. Heat the oil in a wok. Place the bread, shrimp side down, in the oil. When it begins to brown, turn and fry until both sides are golden. Serve immediately.

Note: You may prepare shrimp toast in advance and refrigerate or freeze it. Place on a cooky sheet, and warm in a moderate oven. Do not defrost frozen shrimp toast before warming.

Deep-Fried Chicken

油淋鶏 *(Yu-lin-chi)*

A whole chicken is fried in oil and seasoned. This is a very pretty dish.

4 servings
1 chicken (3 lb.)
Mixture A:
　　2 tablespoons soy sauce
　　1 tablespoon Chinese rice wine or sherry
Mixture B:
　　1 tablespoon minced parsley
　　1 tablespoon minced green onion
　　1 teaspoon minced fresh ginger
　　1 teaspoon minced garlic
　　2½ tablespoons soy sauce
　　2 tablespoons vinegar
　　1 tablespoon Chinese rice wine or sherry
　　1½ tablespoons sugar
canned mandarin oranges, pineapple and
　　cherries for garnish
oil for deep-frying

1. Clean and wash the chicken. Place in boiling water and cook until its color begins to change. Remove and pat dry. Pour Mixture A over it, and let stand for 30 minutes. Drain and dry.
2. Heat a generous amount of oil in a large wok. Deep-fry the chicken, lowering the heat so that it will be cooked through.
3. Cut the chicken right through the bones, into bite-size pieces. Place on a serving dish and pour Mixture B over.
4. Garnish with the canned fruits.

Meatball Stew

砂 鍋 獅 子 頭
(Sha-kuo-shih-tzu-tou)

Eight-treasure Steamed Rice Pudding

八 宝 飯 *(Pa-pao-fan)*

4 servings

1¼ lb. ground pork
1½ lb. Chinese cabbage
1 egg
½ block bean curd
1 tablespoon minced fresh ginger
2 tablespoons minced green onion
Mixture A:
    2½ tablespoons soy sauce
    1½ tablespoons Chinese rice wine
    ½ tablespoon cornstarch
Mixture B:
    ½ teaspoon salt
    2½ tablespoons soy sauce
    1 tablespoon sugar / 1 cup water
cornstarch
a little soy sauce and sugar
3 tablespoons oil

1. Thoroughly combine the ground pork, egg, bean curd, ginger, green onion and Mixture A. Divide into 4 thick patties and dredge with cornstarch.
2. Remove 2 large leaves from the Chinese cabbage. Cut the rest into 1 × 2-inch pieces.
3. Heat the oil in a wok and brown both sides of the meat balls. Remove.
4. Add a pinch of salt to the wok, and stir-fry the sliced Chinese cabbage. Season to taste with soy sauce and sugar.
5. Put one of the large Chinese cabbage leaves on the bottom of a casserole. Place the stir-fried cabbage and meat balls on top, and cover with the other leaf. Pour on Mixture B, and cook over low heat for 30 minutes. Before serving, remove the top leaf.

4 servings

1½ cups glutinous rice, washed and drained
Mixture A:
    2 tablespoons sugar
7 oz. sweet red bean paste
1 tablespoon lard
Mixture B;
    2 tablespoons sugar
    1 tablespoon cornstarch
    1½ cups water
lard or shortening
1 – 1½ cups of mixed fruits and nuts
    (candied walnuts and almonds, ange
    lica, cherries, dried banana, canned
    pineapple, mandarin

1. Cook the glutinous rice in 1½ cups water over medium heat for 15 to 20 minutes, or until water is absorbed. While still hot, combine with Mixture A.
2. Add 1 tablespoon lard to the bean paste, and heat until lard is melted.
3. Grease a heatproof bowl with lard and arrange the fruit and nuts on the bottom. Cut the larger fruits into several decorative pieces.
4. Put half the rice over the fruit and nuts, place the bean paste in the center, and cover with the rest of the rice. Steam for 15 minutes.
5. Heat Mixture B, stirring constantly.
6. When the pudding is steamed, cover the bowl with a plate. Invert the contents of the bowl onto the plate and pour Mixture B over it. If desired, garnish with additional fruit.

111

Crane Appetizer Plate

糖醋蘿蔔 *(T'ang-ts'u-lo-po)*

The crane is a symbol of long life in the Orient.

4 servings

1 Chinese turnip
Mixture A:
  2 tablespoons vinegar
  2 tablespoons sugar
1 small dried Chinese mushroom, soaked
  in water and drained
Mixture B:
  ½ teaspoon soy sauce
  ½ teaspoon sugar
  2 tablespoons water
a snippet of carrot
2 green peas, cooked
salt

1. Carve the neck of the crane from the turnip, as shown in the picture. Then cut off the bottom of the turnip, and cut it in half lengthwise. Make diagonal slits along the curved edges so that they will spread out to form the wings. Cut the leftover pieces of turnip into strips for the body and tail of the bird. Some of the strips should be very thin and others a little thicker for ease in modeling these portions.

2. Pour Mixture A over the pieces of turnip, and let sit for 30 minutes.

3. In a small pan, cook the mushroom in Mixture B.

4. Place the neck of the crane on a serving dish. Build up the body and tail, and place the wings on either side. Use the mushroom for the top of the head, trimming it to fit if necessary. The green peas are the eyes, and the bit of carrot is the bill. Make little slits in the turnip and stick them in.

5. If you have any leftover strips of turnip, form them into flowers. Trimmings from the mushrooms can be used as centers for the flowers.

Fried Chicken and Gingko Nuts

白果鶏丁 *(Pai-kuo-chi-ting)*

The clean green color of the gingko nuts stimulates the appetite.

4 servings
⅔ lb. boneless chicken legs, cut into cubes
Mixture A:
   ½ egg white
   2 teaspoons cornstarch
   2 tablespoons Chinese rice wine or sherry
½ cup gingko nuts, fresh or canned
1 cucumber, peeled and cut into small
   chunks
8 canned cherries
3 tablespoons oil
oil for deep-frying
Mixture B:
   2 tablespoons soy sauce
   1 teaspoon sugar
   2 teaspoons vinegar
a dash of MSG (optional)

1. If using fresh gingko nuts, place in boiling water for 8 minutes. Roast 15 minutes in a heavy frying pan, and peel.
2. Coat the chicken with Mixture A and let sit for 15 minutes.
3. Heat oil for deep-frying in a wok. Deep-fry the chicken until browned. Remove.
4. Heat 3 tablespoons of oil, and add a dash of salt. Stir-fry the cucumber and gingko nuts for 2 minutes. Add the chicken and stir-fry until everything is well cooked.
5. Add Mixture B, and mix together. At the last minute, add the cherries.

Shredded Chicken with Chili Sauce

See p. 25

Steamed Fish

清蒸全魚 *(Ch'ing-chêng-chin-yü)*

Carp as well as red snapper is often prepared this way.

4 servings
1 red snapper (about 1¾ lb.)
4 slices ham, cut into thin strips
½ bamboo shoot, cut into thin strips
3 dried Chinese mushrooms, soaked in
   water and drained, then cut into
   thin strips
Mixture A:
   1 tablespoon lard or shortening
   1 tablespoon Chinese rice wine or sherry
   ½ teaspoon salt
   1 tablespoon vinegar
   1 teaspoon soy sauce
   a pinch of pepper
   a dash of MSG (optional)
1 green onion, cut into thin strips,
   then soaked in cold water
1-inch piece fresh ginger, cut into thin strips

1. Scale, clean and wash the fish. Place it in a large and rather deep heatproof dish, and distribute the ham, bamboo shoot and mushrooms over the surface. Pour over Mixture A.
2. Steam over high heat for 20 minutes or until cooked.
3. Transfer the fish to a serving dish. Sprinkle with the onion and ginger strips around the fish.

Deep-Fried Rice Flour Balls
蔴 球 *(Ma-ch'iu)*

4 servings
1 lb. rice flour (about 3-⅔ cups)
½ lb. sweet red bean paste
1 package white sesame seeds
½ cup sugar / red food coloring
2 lettuce leaves
oil for frying

1. Gradually add lukewarm water to the rice flour until the dough has the consistency of your ear lobe. Knead it well and divide into 8 to 10 balls.
2. Divide the bean paste into the same number of pieces as the dough, and form into balls.
3. Flatten the rice flour balls between the palms of your hands. Wrap these circles of dough around the bean paste. Dredge with sesame seeds.
4. Heat the oil to 210°F to 300°F and carefully deep-fry the balls, turning them over occasionally until they double in size. While they are frying, prick 2 small holes in them with a skewer.
5. Mix enough food coloring with the sugar to make a pretty shade of pink.
6. Place the balls on a bed of lettuce, using your fingers, sprinkle them with the tinted sugar.

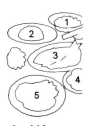

1. Fried Chicken and Gingko Nuts, p. 114
2. Shredded Chicken with Chili Sauce, p. 25
3. Steamed Fish, p. 114
4. Deep-Fried Rice Flour Balls, p. 115
5. Triple-Combination Appetizer, p. 115

◀p. 113

Triple-Combination Appetizer
三 拼 盤 *(San-p'in-p'an)*

4 servings
½ chicken, washed and rinsed with boiling water
Mixture A:
  ½ cup soy sauce / ½ cup water
  1 tablespoon Chinese rice wine or sherry
  1 green onion / 1-inch piece fresh ginger
1 tablespoon sugar
2 cucumbers, quartered lengthwise and seeds removed, then cut into 2-inches.
2-inches piece carrot, quartered lengthwise
1 teaspoon salt
1-inch piece fresh ginger, cut into thin strips
2 tablespoons oil
3 chili peppers, seeded
2 tablespoons sugar / 2 tablespoons vinegar
1 canned abalone, cut into 2-inch-slices
several sprigs of parsley

1. Heat Mixture A in a saucepan. Place the chicken in it and cook over moderate heat, turning occasionally. When the chicken can be easily pierced with a fork or skewer, add the sugar and cook for another 5 minutes. Remove from the heat, and let cool in the saucepan then slice the chicken.
2. Sprinkle the cucumbers and carrot with the salt. Set aside for 30 minutes. Drain. Place in a bowl and top with the strips of ginger.
3. Heat the oil in a wok and stir-fry the chili peppers. Add the sugar and vinegar to make a sweet-and-soy sauce. Pour the sauce over the vegetables, and set aside for half a day.
4. Arrange the chicken, vegetables and abalone on a serving dish. Garnish with parsley.

CHINESE WINE

CHINESE WINE

Various districts of China are noted for their locally produced wines. Unlike Western wines, which are pressed from grapes, most Chinese wines are distilled from grains such as glutinous rice, wheat or *kao-liang*. Some are very mild; others are as strong as or stronger than whisky and brandy.

Chinese wines differ from Western alcoholic beverages in the manner in which they are served. Western drinks often have special functions—the before-dinner cocktail, the after-dinner liqueur, red wine with meat and white wine with fish, etc. You may forget about these distinctions with Chinese wines. Find one that you like, and drink it anytime—before, during and after the meal.

Standard Wines

Shao-hsing-chiu 紹興酒   (Chekiang District)
This area is noted for its delicious water, and the wine produced from it is the basic Chinese table and cooking wine. It contains 20% alcohol.

When *shao-hsing* wine is made, it is put in a jar and is usually buried in the ground for 3–4 years to ripen. The longer it is left underground, the better the taste is supposed to be. In northern China, people often drink it with rock sugar. Southern Chinese drink it plain. There is a tradition that whenever a girl is born, her family makes *shao-hsing* wine and buries it. On the girl's wedding day, the wine is exhumed and is drunk at the wedding party. Substitutions: For cooking, Japanese *sake*, dry sherry (never cream or cooking sherry), gin or Sauterne. For drinking, *sake*. To serve, slightly warm both *shao-hsing* wine and *sake*, and pour into tiny Oriental drinking cups or liqueur glasses.

Mao-t'ai-chiu 茅台酒   (Kweichow District)
Mao-t'ai wine is made from the distillation of *kao-liang* and wheat. It is a transparent

wine with a wonderful aroma and is so strong (the alcohol content is 53% to 55%) that it easily catches on fire.

Chu-yeh-ch'ing-chiu 竹葉青酒 (Kwangsi District)
Bamboo leaves are steeped in this wine, giving it the flavor and green color of the leaves. It contains 45% alcohol.

Kao-liang-chiu 高粱酒 (Hupeh District)
This wine is similar to gin and vodka in its transparency, but is much stronger (58% to 62% alcohol content.)

Sweet Wine and Women's Drinks

Kuei-hua-ch'en-chiu 桂花陳酒 (Peking District)
Osmanthus petals and buds are steeped in this wine, and then it is stored for 3 years. It is very tasty and is at its best when served chilled. The alcohol content is 11% to 14%.

Mei-kuei-la-chiu 玫瑰露酒 (Peking District)
This wine has a strong aroma and a sweet taste. The alcohol content is 52% to 56%.

Ch'ing-mei-chiu 青梅酒 (Canton District)
This is a sweet plum brandy.

Medical Wines

Wu-chia-p'i-chiu 五加皮酒 (Canton District)
Twenty spices are added to this wine which has the beautiful red color of safflower. It contains many nutrients and is famous as a health drink. The alcohol content is 53% to 54%.

Ke-chieh-ta-pu-chiu 蛤蚧大補酒 (Canton District)
This wine contains extracts from snakes, deer horn and carrots. The alcohol content is 37%.

Hu-ku-chiu 虎骨酒 (Canton District)
This wine has been made for hundreds of years. It contains and incredible 140 kinds of spices, as well as deer horn, a tiger's bone and carrots. Good as a cure for neuralgia, it contains 50% alcohol.

Jen-shen-chiu 人参酒 (Chi-lin District)
This wine is made from a special distillation of carrots and contains many nutrients. The alcohol content is 39% to 40%.

Seating Arrangement

The Chinese base their seating arrangements on the fact that their houses are usually built facing the south and on their preference for round tables. If your house faces some other direction and your dining table is rectangular, you may have to modify the eating plan. The seat facing the south and/or the entrance is reserved for the guest of honor. The other seats are distributed to people according to their degree of closeness to him.
No one should sit down before the guest of honor sits down, and no one should stand up at the end of the meal before he stands.
The guest of honor serves himself first.
In China, when there is no guest of honor, the seating arrangement is decided according to age.

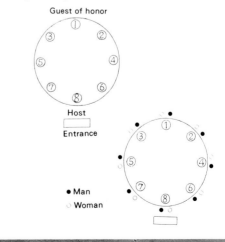

TIPS ABOUT COOKING WITH OIL

How to check for quality

The oil should be light-colored, clear and glossy. It should not have a strong smell. If it has any oder at all, it should smell subtly "like itself" —that is, olive oil smells like olives, etc.

When heated, there should be no offensive odor, smoke or foam.

How to prepare deep-frying oil for re-use

Strain through cheesecloth or a very fine wire mesh.

Pour into a bottle or other container with a close-fitting cover, seal tightly and store in a cool, dark place.

Special tips for deep-frying

NEW OIL will fry food to a very light finish. First, deep-fry the ingredients in just enough oil to allow them to cook, then add more oil bit by bit to the center. This procedure keeps the oil fresher for later re-use.

USED OIL should be combined with an equal amount of new oil.

Eventually, oil that has been used and re-used will not produce foods with a fine finish. But you may still use this oil again when frying dumplings.

How to check the temperature of oil

A thermometer, of course, gives the most accurate information about temperature. If you don't have a thermometer, drop a pinch of flour into the oil and observe what happens:

If the flour doesn't rise instantly from the bottom, the temperature is under 320°F.

The flour will rise instantly at 320°F.

If the flour doesn't reach the bottom before rising, and if it rises from the center, the temperature is 340°F-350°F.

If the flour doesn't sink at all, but spreads out over the surface of the oil, the temperature is approximately 390°F.

TIP: If you put too many ingredients in the oil at the same time, the temperature of the oil will drop down and the food will not be as crispy.

SAMPLE MENUS

Family Meal
I
Beef and Pickled Mustard GreenSoup
Canton Style Egg Fu Yong
Tomato and Cucumber Salad

II
Chicken Casserole
Bean Sprouts Salad
Deep-Fried Eggplant "Sandwiches"

Holiday Gathering
Deep-Fried Fish Sticks
Ground Meat and Egg Custard
Chicken Wings with Vegetables
Stewed Chinese Cabbage and Mushrooms

Birthday Party
Shrimp Toast
Sweet and Sour Pork
Meatball Stew
Soft Fried Noodles
Bean Jam Buns
Vegetable Soup

Christmas Buffet
Meatball and Soybean Stew
Deep-Fried Wrapped Beef
Family Style Roast Pork
Four Colored Shao-mai
Ham and Chicken in Noodles Soup
Almond Jelly

Chinese Flavorings and Spices

Chi-ma-chiang
芝蔴醬
(Hot Sesame Seed Sauce)

A mixture of toasted and ground sesame seeds and sesame oil. Used in dressings for vegetable salads and as a seasoning for noodles.

Chiang-tou-fu
醬豆腐
(Fermented Bean Curd)

A preserve of bean curd, salt and spices, which has been allowed to ferment. It has either a creamy or dark red color and is used as a flavoring for simmered foods. Sold in small jars, cans or bottles.

La-chiao-chiang
辣椒醬
(Hot Bean Paste)

A mixture of bean paste and red peppers. It is red with a very thick consistency, and is very hot. Used in fried foods and hors d'oeuvre.

La-yu
辣油
(Hot Sauce)

A mixture of sesame oil and red peppers, heated slowly until the oil becomes spicy. Used in spring rolls and steam-fried dumplings and other fried foods and noodles.

Hao-yu
蠔油
(Oyster Sauce)

A sauce produced by combining oyster broth with soy sauce. Used for fried foods or as a table sauce.

Hsia-yu
蝦油
(Shrimp Sauce)

A sauce produced through the fermentation of finely ground shrimps. Has a very strong odor but is appetizing.

Pa-chiao
八角
(Star Anise)

Fennel. The black nutlet can be seen within the husk which opens like a flower. The aroma of this spice destroys any strong odor of fish or other meat. Often used in boiled and fried foods.

Hua-chiao
花椒
(Szechwan Pepper or Flower Pepper)

Szechwan pepper seeds, used for boiled meat and pickled vegetables. It has a pungent aroma and somewhat bitter taste.

Hua-chiao-yen
花椒塩

A mixture of toasted and ground Szechwan pepper and salt, which has been thoroughly dried and sifted. Used for deep-fried foods, meat and fish.

Wu-hsian-fên
五香粉
(Five Spices Powder)

A ground mixture of anise seed, Szechwan pepper, cloves, cinnamon and dried tangerine peel. Used in the preparation of meat stew or steamed meat and smoked fish.

NOTE: These spices and flavorings may be found at food specialty stores, Japanese grocery stores and in any Chinatown.

Index

About the Author

Madam Constance D. Chang is an authority on Chinese Cooking, wildely known for her delicious Chinese food, for her easy-to-follow-recipes, and her willingness and ability to impart her knowledge to others.

At present, Mrs. Chang owns and operates or directly supervises seven Chinese restaurants in Japan. Four restaurants under her supervision are in hotels owned by the Tokyu Hotel Company, of which she is director. They are each known as the "Peacock Hall" and are located in Tokyo, Yokohama and Fukuoka, and at the Haneda (Tokyo) International Airport. She owns and operates three independent Chinese restaurants in Tokyo, each named "Madam Chang's Home Kitchen," located in the Shibuya, Setagaya and Ochanomizu districts. Mrs. Chang is the author of a variety of cookbooks on Chinese and Japanese cooking. Her books have been published in Hong Kong, Tokyo, London, New York, San Francisco and Hawaii in Chinese, Japanese and English, in all of which she is fluent and with translations into German, Dutch and Portuguese. For more than 20 years she has appeared on the Japanese national TV network (NHK) and local TV stations with her Chinese cooking instructions. She is now engaged in the conduct of four cooking classes in Tokyo. First, there is her own cooking school in Ochanomizu. She supervises the Chinese portion of the multinational cooking class sponsored by the Asahi News Company, in the Asahi Cultural Center, and a class sponsored by the Shufunotomo Company, one of Japan's most prestigious publishing houses. Finally, she conducts a class known as the "Better Home" School of cooking.

Mrs. Chang is famous for having initiated the first Chinese buffet-style restaurants in Japan; they are quite likely the first in the world!

Madame Chang's cookbooks are illustrated with full color photographs of the various dishes, and with many original sketches. The latter are a natural outgrowth of the artistry of this intrepid lady, who is widely recongnized for her Chinese paintings and calligraphy.